DREAMSTORM P

BADASS AFFIRMATIONS
FOR WOMEN

DOWNLOAD YOUR FREE GIFT

Introducing **"The Badass Woman's Toolkit for Positive Transformation"** - your personal treasure trove of empowerment, designed exclusively for the woman who's ready to stand tall, shine bright, and embrace her awesomeness.

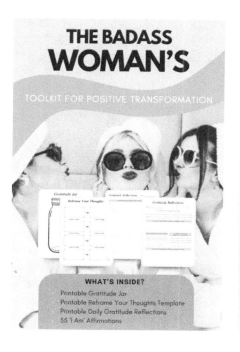

What's Inside This Magical Toolbox?

- Printable Gratitude Jar

- Printable Reframe Your Thoughts Template

- Printable Daily Gratitude Reflections

- 55 'I Am' Affirmations

Your journey to becoming the best version of yourself begins now. Scan this QR code and say goodbye to days dimmed by doubt, and hello to a life lit with self-empowerment.

A girl should be two things: who and what she wants.

COCO CHANEL

A girl should be two things: who and what she wants.

CONTENTS

INTRODUCTION

Grace ever so gently pushed aside the book of affirmations with trembling hands, and that act was sufficient to give Bailee a glimpse of the tremors surging inside her best friend. "You are handing me a pair of hyper skates when I don't have a skating rink," Grace remarked wistfully, trying to keep her voice from cracking. Bailee glanced at her treasured handbook, whose pages had yellowed from years of use. It seemed to be communicating, telling her to be patient and allow Grace to vent her pain. Bailee's heart went out to her best buddy. She could not miss the lack of hope in her voice. Her colleague of nine years and dear friend was the most unlikely candidate expected to need help in coming to terms with her feelings and in seeing meaning in her life. On the face of it, she appeared to have all she needed, so to speak. But right at this moment, it was as if she had suddenly woken up and realized she had spent all these years living the wrong life. She came from a highly accomplished family, graduated from an Ivy League college, and was married to a good man who was clearly in love with her. Nicholas ticked all the boxes for an ideal family man. He was extremely caring towards Grace and a devoted father to their two daughters. He was not chauvinistic by any means, as he held her opinions in high respect. Furthermore, he was doing well, boasting impressive academic accomplishments and a successful professional career. But something was troubling her in their marriage. As much as she tried to put her finger on it, she could not point out anything specific.

Bailee's leather-covered collection of affirmations matured like aged rum, carved out of the deepest tribulations of women across time and cultures. Insights that flashed and solutions that sprang to life from the excruciating pains of life lay on the dusky mahogany table between them. Bailee knew that it held the secret weapons that would help Grace brace herself on her path to self-awareness. But Grace was hurting so badly that it prevented her from accepting the help she desperately needed.

Not that they hadn't discussed it previously. Listening to Grace, Bailee deduced that her problems were caused by the fact that Grace lacked a certain autonomy in her marriage. She instinctively knew that Grace was in search of that freedom of spirit that is every individual's fundamental need. She suggested that Nicholas perhaps has a domineering personality, which was why she felt invalidated. This was met with vehement resistance and denial. "Bailee, how could you even suggest such a thing?" blurted out Grace, visibly hurt. Bailee did not react; she had to allow Grace time for that perspective to sink in. Bailee knew her one statement would not cut through deeply ingrained cultural conditioning. It would take time!

"You are fine as you are, Grace. It is the world that needs healing," Bailee mused as she picked up her glass of warm cinnamon mocha. Grace looked up with a frown. "Your annoying comment got me intrigued," she said finally. Bailee was expecting this invitation to the coffee shop this cold Saturday evening, for she knew what she said had hit home.

Can We Upset the Self-Defeating Mental Chatter?

The idea that individuals are victims of society is not an overstatement. Years of conditioning have made us believe that our family and friends are always giving us sound advice and have our best interests. We look at our gut feelings with suspicion, and we become our gaslighter in the process. And when life throws its inevitable obstacles at us, we fall into our traps and struggle for solutions. In other words, Grace was suffering the maladies of a patriarchal society where she was losing autonomy to her partner in an extremely subtle way. Bailee wished for Grace to open her eyes to it.

The "whispering self" was the term used and can be described as a continuous internal dialogue within each of us (Purkey, 2002). The takeaway is that it is possible to monitor and direct our dialogues within us in positive ways. New beliefs can replace old ones. This is very similar to the principle of the growth mindset, which establishes that our intelligence is not pre-set and is very much malleable. Yes, training and self-awareness play an important part in tapping into one's potential and converting the possibility into reality. There is no magic pill, and neither is the process of child's play.

In his work, *The Genius In All Of Us*, David Shenk (2011) observes how children of low-income households undergo greater amounts of rejections than those of high-income families. He notes that among other obvious advantages, hearing positive things about themselves helps advantaged children succeed far more than growing up not hearing as many optimistic beliefs. Thankfully, as adults, each one of us gets our chance to change our script, if necessary, through positive affirmations. Affirmations help create these internal dialogues based on respecting and loving the self and others, creating self-assurance, and helping see the world through an "I am okay and so are you" lens. Affirmations support the basic assumption that people are reasonable by nature and the world is a safe place. Of course, we will have enough instances to prove this assumption wrong, but that's where we need to release ourselves from an imprisoning narrative. Developing the ability to understand where the other person's behavior is coming from is a skill worth cultivating. It saves time and energy.

HOW TO USE THIS BOOK

I will not claim to entirely know how. But what I am sure of is that it is not a one-time reading-feeling happy-putting away piece of work. It comes alive when used as a daily reference in the reflection mode. When you look at yourself as a collaborator with equal ownership of the work and not just a reader is when the book begins to breathe. Be assured that every sentence you read will have a different meaning at another time. So the hope is that this book grows and evolves with you. Like the universe, it will take a step toward you as you take yours toward it. Understanding the basis on which affirmations have survived over centuries and are thriving as the world gets more multi-layered sets one in the right frame of mind to take it forward and not give up midway. I owe my reader a caveat. Affirmations as a practice could look difficult or even pointless initially. You will be amazed to see the practice come alive as you dig deeper. But the other side of latching on is a different story, and hence worth the initial struggles and skepticism.

Once the why is internalized, go on to adopt the various paths to practice them one at a time. Tap into your powerful creative energies with the help of the prompts present in every line of the book. Reading real-life accounts of individuals who have triumphed through a variety of challenges will help you comprehend the underlying message and, more importantly, develop your perspective on it. Because once we learn to create our own happiness, no force can take it away from us.

The layout facilitates the daily application of the principles and practices distilled from a myriad of sources cutting across time and cultures. Go on, modify and refine the affirmations to match your unique context using them as the reference points. This book adores a reader who has the curiosity of a child and will gladly become their companion. Happy Discovery!

Chapter One:
THE POWER OF AFFIRMATIONS

Statements that show us the right direction in the turmoil of life are like the sails of a ship on choppy waters. The sails have to work to save the ship, so would it not be worthwhile for every captain to invest in good quality, effective ones? Sounds like common sense. But this knowledge alone is not sufficient to have.

Affirmations Are Not for Everyone Though

It requires you to first acknowledge that YOU are the captain. Only then will you even bother to take action to address the sails. We have long been imbued with the belief that we are not very capable of changing things in our own lives and that we must strive to earn the respect and approval of others. The smartest and the most educated of us fall unwittingly into this trap. It takes us a lot of time to even realize that we conveniently believe we have no control over our lives. All this conditioning by society, culture, and well-intentioned parents from the moment we are born is deeply ingrained in our subconscious. Admittedly, it is not easy to wash away our personality. It is hard work and can get frustrating at times. But have faith because the rewards you get in terms of life satisfaction and fulfillment are immeasurable. So remember, you will see meaning in investing in sails ONLY if you believe you are the captain. If you believe you are just one of the passengers whose destiny is a factor in how others manage the ship, well, you will not lose much. Life will go on, getting battered by the winds and the waters. After a while, you may become numb to the pain. But the question is, is there not a better choice? What do you think is the way out?

It May Not Feel Right Initially, and It's Going to Be Clumsy, but It Is Worth the Struggle

Be prepared to feel foolish during the initial days. Allow the process to evolve before you decide it is a waste of time. We are creatures of conditioning, and the mind hates getting challenged. So be prepared for massive resistance. The right affirmations will show us clear direction, and that evasive sense of triumph will surrender to you. It may take longer, but you get better at orienting your mind with experience. Remember that people spend a lifetime carrying resentment and anger in their hearts. It is common—so common that it has become normalized. Do you want to be like the vast majority, or do you have the courage to want to live an extraordinary life? The choice is yours.

Just like exercise, affirmation is also seen as unnatural by the human brain. Research has established that the human body naturally wants to conserve energy, and we have not evolved to indulge in physical activity that is not perceived by the brain as needed for survival (Liberman, 2020). Going for that daily walk or doing strength training can only be a deliberate act because we know that it is good for us.

Affirmations also work on similar lines. It is an unnatural process that we need to consciously indulge in because it helps. Unless the intention is to reset every single day, it would not mean anything to you. Saying it out loud and feeling good about it will also take some time. Do not worry about feeling awkward. The conviction will come in time as you stay with it and begin to see the change for yourself.

Affirmations Open the Pathways to Realization of Truth

They replace the generations-long brainwashing that makes up our unfair, "might makes right" society. Every time we find ourselves unable to move past a challenging circumstance, we have the opportunity to reconsider our deeply embedded belief structures. Maybe something's getting in the way, something needs to be unlearned, or something needs to be added in terms of life skills. We find ourselves in the difficult situation of having to consciously reframe these values and reject popular culture. We get our new language through affirmations, and the process will undoubtedly take time.

It Helps Us Overcome the Tricks Our Minds Play on Us

Here is an exercise that we should indulge in now and then: Pause and reflect on statements we make, positions we take, assumptions we bake, and attitudes we fake. It helps point fingers at the cultural biases we have. Daniel Kahneman, the winner of the Nobel Prize in Economics, successfully pointed to the many biases and heuristics we hold while making decisions (Kahneman, 2011). Much as we like to think otherwise, most of our super-important decisions and judgments are taken based on feelings and not rational thinking. This observation had huge repercussions on our understanding of how economics and politics work; it is only a guess that it impacts our daily life and relationships.

Affirmations Are Not About Putting up a Brave Face While Struggling Inside

It would not be worthwhile to try and prove or disprove it to be a science or belief, for they are truths that cannot be boxed into frameworks. We need to look at it through the lens of wisdom, and it works only if it works! It is not going to make you feel perfect or invincible. It is not a sword with which you vanquish your adversaries with your sharp wit or comebacks. Affirmations give you back the peace of mind you deserve by making your values and ethics work for you. We do not use affirmations to live in denial, wishing away our realities. We use affirmations to face our demons and be mindful of the choices we have. Nor are they winning cards for gaining one-upmanship in an ego battle. They are our allies in seeking the truth that will liberate our minds from ignorance.

It Is Not About Nurturing Toxic Positivity

We have seen them as characters in movies. Sometimes we come across people in our lives who are annoyingly cheerful. Your gut would tell you something is out of place even if you are not able to define why they put us off. Invalidating the emotions of others and not being mindful of the moods of others is no different from hiding dust under the carpet.

How Do Affirmations Work?

Will they even occur to me when my mind is in turmoil? Are they just feel-good statements that do not have long-term effects? Are you skeptical about affirmations? If yes, you are on the right track. Approaching it with a critical mind will help one dig deeper and get it right. If not, it will be one of the many feel-good self-help pieces of advice that don't stick.

It Retrieves the Right File from Your Life to Solve an Existing Problem

If you couldn't get the tea leaves out of your fully stocked cupboard, could you still pour yourself a cup of tea? The several spice bottles that are easily accessible wouldn't help, surely. Affirmations are an effective strategy to match the problem to the right solution that is right within you! Think of an embarrassing moment in your life, something you wish did not happen. Replaying that memory over and over again will put you in a state of self-doubt when you have to make a completely unrelated decision in the future. Add to it the fact that we readily recollect negative incidents, thanks to the brain's strong survival instinct.

But we are more than our instincts. Human beings have a thinking brain that can choose a response that goes against instinct. This ability serves a useful purpose. We can train ourselves, with some effort, to choose the appropriate emotions that emerge in a given situation. Affirmations do the work of zooming in on the right memories to whip up the emotion that is needed at the given moment. For instance, if the present circumstances are making you feel like a failure, you will dive into the file with memories of your strength. Though we don't recall them as easily as failures, there are those moments when we did things that we are so proud of. Those are the memories we need to equip us with the confidence to deal with this one. Once the mindset shifts successfully, one would find the problem magically getting reframed as well. Experience one, and there will be no turning back!

From a Psychological Perspective, It Helps to Unlearn and Rewire

A psychologist or a scientific paper will decipher the working of the mind and talk about understanding human behavior. But the subject appears so complex, and a person facing a real-life challenge may be lost on where to begin the process of implementing theory into effective practice. This is where common sense practices like affirmations come to the rescue. It helps one prepare the mind to work in a sensible direction. Focusing or channeling our thoughts in a particular direction helps strengthen the neuroplasticity of the brain for a certain outcome. Neuroplasticity is the ability of our brain to rewire. We direct the mind towards positivity and empowerment because when left alone, it veers towards negativity and self-defeating thoughts as part of this defense mechanism. This happens because our brain prefers to look at everything as a threat so that it can fight or flee to safety.

Affirmations, in a sense, trick the brain into coming out of the fight-or-flight mode so that logic and reasoning can take over. We can make smart decisions only when the brain allows us to. The practice helps create an image in your mind of the desired outcome, leading us to work towards achieving it. Want it, and the universe will conspire towards it, as they say. An affirmation trains us to give words to emotions, especially negative ones. Have you ever felt your heartbeat race or your mind get agitated when a person you can't stand walks in or calls you up? Common, right? But it does not occur to us that others around us feel the same for us, fairly or unfairly. Anyway, it helps get back our control when we can convert our agitation into a sentence such as "I am feeling nervous" or "My blood is boiling." This will help you come up with an antidote affirmation almost immediately. Replace the statement with thoughts like "I do not fall into stupidity traps," "Others cannot control my emotions," or "I understand that their narcissistic behavior is coming out of self-loathing."

What I am doing is enough. I am a kind human being.

Chapter Two:
THE ART OF MAKING AFFIRMATIONS WORK

eeßßßßee

You need a time of your choosing to completely zone into yourself. It could be morning, afternoon, night, or midnight. It depends on your frame of mind in the present moment. Just as a captivating movie or Netflix series transports us into a different world, and its effect lingers on for days to come and sometimes brings profound changes in our very core we need to achieve a shift, except that we must direct our own life this time. Why? Because there is no one else coming to direct it for you. All that is being asked of you, by you, is 15 minutes a day. Pick the most important 15 minutes of your day with deliberation.

Be Brutally Honest About Self-Limiting Beliefs

The first step is to work toward self-awareness. Keep in mind that it is not easy because your brain is going to trick you into believing things that are not true. Our ego does play an active part too. Nobody likes to be told they are wrong. Whenever a tiny voice from your consciousness tells you to reconsider your opinion on something or someone, the ego will immediately resist with very logical and grand-sounding theories explaining why your wrong thinking is right. So sit it out and take your time to reflect, have conversations about it with people you respect, and take your time to objectively assess the situation and the steps you need to take. It is always better than jumping at the first impulse that comes to you. Your initial hunch could be true. Reflection helps even then because you are now better equipped with strategies to deal with it, and you will also forgive yourself if mistakes get committed in the process.

The Spoken Sentences

When spoken aloud, it will help control what goes into your thoughts. We are what we think, right? Harbor negative thoughts, and you see negative things around that further reinforce the bias. Replace it with reasonable thoughts, and you will see the reality shift almost magically. Use sentences that help design your life for the better and keep it away from getting swung into random and wild directions. Using them in the present tense (*I am strong*) affirms that it is the truth as opposed to the future tense (*I will be strong*) since it only indicates a possibility or a potential. That is when you get to experience the strength that you seek in you. Your body, mind, and spirit will feel the strength already, and this will attract what you are looking for. Use the phrases *I understand* (I understand that people can be ignorant), *I love* (I love in abundance in my life), *I speak* (I speak strength and power), *I do* (I attract the right people), *I feel* (I feel wealthy and powerful), and *I see* (I see the needs of others), along with *I am* phrase to make the affirmations multi-dimensional and hence exponentially enhance its effectiveness.

Use the power of the spoken word to channel your precious energy. We know that words expressed are exponentially more effective than thoughts that fleet in mind. They come alive when spoken. Speak them out loud every day, and you will see them stirring up a different reality. It helps in monitoring your emotions. Negative feelings can be countered with positive affirmations spoken loudly. Replace the thought My job sucks with the affirmation *I will protect my peace by doing my work with all sincerity.* This will get you to discover the joys of working with a fresh attitude or will provide you with the motivation to seek better opportunities. Either way, you find a way out of the misery.

The Elephant and the Rider

It is perplexing why it is so damn difficult to practice what we preach. We all seem to know what is to be done, but it feels impossible to follow up on what we need to do. Jonathan Haidt (2006) put it in perspective in his highly acclaimed work *The Happiness Hypothesis*, followed by Chip and Dan Heath (2010) in their work *Switch: How to Change Things When Change is Hard.* The analogy of the elephant and the rider was used to explain the reason for the dilemma. It suggests that we all have two parts of the mind: the first part, like the rider of an elephant, is the rational thinker who knows what is right and wrong, and the second part is the elephant, who is emotional, stronger, and which works on autopilot. The elephant is the part that refuses to come out of the warm blanket when the rider has decided that early morning walks are good for health. The summary is that we need to train the elephant every day, gently and consistently, as reasoning does not appeal to it.

Daily Is the Way to Go

The mind will not whip up courage and conviction out of the blue if your conditioning has been otherwise. It takes time to practice and prepare for the storms. Small steps every day is the only way to detangle the mixed-up mind and make it razor-sharp with helpful beliefs. Aspects of looking inside of us and knowing oneself have got buried in the industrialized education system. The world got busy studying the outside, and hence knowing the insides of us and our spirituality got sidelined. We are now paying the price with increased mental health issues and a lack of resilience rampant across generations. But the great news is that we know what is to be done. Never in society has there been such openness in talking about our deepest feelings and fears. Age-old practices that have withstood the test of time are being relooked into before dismissing them altogether. One cannot tame a wild elephant just like that unless there is daily nudging and prodding. It is the slow and steady process of chipping away old ways and substituting with new ways that is going to begin the process of change.

Not Mindless Repetition

What we are looking for are everyday opportunities to create the required actions and emotions within us. Saying you are a self-sufficient person and then giving into your boss's atrocious work demands because you have a promotion at stake are incongruous moves. It is something that will make you fall in your own eyes and eventually hurt your self-esteem. Reminding yourself every day that you are a self-sufficient person should give you the willpower to take a dignified stand. You will, at some point or the other, keep losing faith in the affirmation. That is completely acceptable and is a natural process. As long as you are coming back to it, it is working well. It takes time before your affirmation will begin to unravel your strengths. It essentially prepares your mind to receive higher wisdom and worldly achievements. Complete the affirmative sentence with your story following it. *I am wonderful* should be followed by thinking of how you felt when you helped that friend when you were a little girl. Even if it seems like a small thing, follow up the affirmation with actions that demonstrate the intention.

Pulling Out Your Story From Deep Within

Listening to Patrick Bet-David (Valuetainment, 2019) was a revelation. It's wonderful how he makes his affirmations effective. His insights came from years of figuring out the best ways to make it work. When he says that statements are effective when they highlight the moments in your own life when the emotions of pain, success, and invincibility hit you particularly hard, he is dead on. He advises writing down your most painful experiences, the most upsetting criticism you have heard, and the times when you felt especially proud of your choices and actions. Connect them to your affirmations and watch them come alive. To tie them to the affirmations that you want to work for you, you must find them among the countless thoughts, memories, and perceptions that fill your mind. If you can think of a time when you surprised yourself by overcoming a challenge, your present internal dialogue that says you are free from other people's opinions will have more value. You purposefully go to the moment in your life where you felt the emotion that you need now, very much like actors tapping into their arsenal of stories and emotions to whip out that perfect take, says Patrick to articulate how the affirmation is brought to life. It taps the right emotion from your own story and gives you the confidence to say, "I've done it before, so I can do it again," which will help the affirmation stick. It generates the energy that only repeating a sentence will not provide you with. Change your sentences if you have to, scrap them even, until you find something that connects deep within you. Face your fears, be bold, and have fun!

Association of the Senses

Another way to reign the monkey brain is to take advantage of its appeal for habit. We are creatures of habit and, therefore, will not get out of the house without brushing our teeth, even if we don't consciously think of the relevance of oral hygiene. It helps to build a ritual so that we don't miss out on reinforcing our affirmations daily. Keep an alarm, light a candle, use meditation bowls, bells, and incense sticks, have an affirmation corner, or combine it with your morning coffee. Combine them with powerful body language, like keeping a regal posture, giving yourself a thumbs up, and saying a loud cheer. Go ahead, figure out, and do what it takes to get you to stick to the practice. Something undoubtedly stirs up when you do your affirmation in front of the mirror, looking into your eyes. This is perhaps because we cannot deceive ourselves and can only say what we mean, and there is a transfer of powerful energy into the self in the process.

Create Ones That Are Meaningful to Your Life Circumstance

If the affirmation is beautiful in itself and the divine truth, it would still be ineffective or feel inauthentic if it is not specific to your challenge. Very generic statements alone will feel fake when you say them, and you feel the friction when you say them out loud. "I do not scroll aimlessly" would be too generic. But "I keep my phone in another room while working" sounds more resolute and action-oriented.

For the affirmations to seem credible, try to be as explicit as possible. A few trials and errors will surely get you there. Keep at it, and soon you will be good to go. The affirmation should give you a surge of passion and strength for action every time you say one. Otherwise, it would be an ineffective pill that you swallow mindlessly. If you want an impact, genuineness is the key. Even a general-sounding affirmation such as "I am not lazy" should be accompanied by savoring a memory where you were rewarded for taking that first bold step towards something that you kept procrastinating. The emotion that accompanies the statement is what makes the affirmation complete.

Letting Go And Trusting

There is no breathing in without breathing out, and happiness cannot be defined in the absence of sadness. Skepticism is a good place to begin with because blind faith will stop you from searching for any deep meaning. Constantly thinking about the affirmations will tire you out. It would be like taking antibiotics every day, rendering it ineffective when it is needed. Watching cooking shows 17 hours a day does not do what half an hour of cooking does. Say your affirmations intentionally during the designated time and let go of them from your conscious mind. Walk around free, for you have entrusted the job of your well-being to life forces. For once you have placed your trust, the Universe has your back, having taken up the task of loving, protecting, and guiding you.

Improvising on the Go

Much like everything organic, it evolves. We have to make the sentences personal and relevant. The trouble sometimes is that we deny ourselves the opportunities to learn and unlearn. We like predictability and look for patterns to follow blindly. The practice needs to be constant, much like a skeletal framework on which the muscles can move freely. For instance, no one could take away my morning reflection time, not even me. I would sit in my bed even on days I just did not feel like it. But my affirmations would constantly keep morphing until I genuinely felt them coming from my soul.

Chapter Three:
STORIES OF WOMEN
WHO ARE THRIVING

"The nature of thoughts that came flooding into my mind in the mornings began to change... and that was my first experience of a miracle," said Linda. No one missed the radiance in her voice and the relief on her face. "It took me about two months of following them to even notice any change."

Each of our stories and circumstances is unique. But very interestingly, all of them have an underlying motif that can be identified to diagnose the problem. This makes it possible to arrive at solutions because now we are working with fundamental principles that are shared universally. Much as we look towards famous people for their inspirational stories of having overcome personal challenges to defy social norms that kill our spirit, it helps to see traces of them in people all around us. It is not surprising that a marginalized, disadvantaged woman can demonstrate life lessons to a privileged, entitled person struggling with a life lesson. Sometimes, all it takes is to slow down and observe. Because sometimes, we are not looking for successes to announce to the world. All one would need is to look proudly into the mirror every morning.

Talking about instances the contemporary woman faces will help us figure out the underlying patterns and thus put each one of us in a position to strategize effectively. Another's insights can serve as our torchlight when navigating a world full of broken people. The weapons we need are not self-pity, disgust, and resentment but wisdom, empathy, and leadership. The toughest obstacle usually is convincing ourselves of this reality.

Surviving Difficult People

My Stability Calms Down Any Turbulence That Comes My Way

In Linda's cultural setting, the mother-in-law was part of the package in the marriage. In her society, though outwardly, people lived their independent lives, the mother-in-law vicariously tagged along with her expectations. The instincts of possessiveness, control, and resentment somehow found a way into Linda's marriage. It did not matter that the couple did not stay in the same house or country. For Linda, deciphering and navigating her mother-in-law's seemingly innocent suggestions took an emotional toll. Her muscles would tighten and trigger a headache every time the lady called. Her mother-in-law would talk very sweetly, which only highlighted the passive aggression in the tone. Her moves had to be regularly dissected and checked for manipulation because they would find ways of swaying her husband's emotions. Linda resented the unfair control, but her effort to talk it out with her husband hit a dead end every time because of his inability to empathize with her situation. His upbringing did not help him understand her position vis-a-vis his mother. He could not see why she was getting worked up and, at best, lost patience with Linda for pushing the envelope unnecessarily.

Setting boundaries was the biggest challenge for Linda. She knew that people would be quick to label her, and she had to steel herself for it. Her initial hesitations about rocking the boat gave way to polite but clear lines laid on her husband's family. If her husband was initially taken aback by her behavior, he gradually came to respect her viewpoint. Things changed for Linda the moment she overcame her victim mentality and stopped being a people pleaser. Finally, she had given herself permission to be firm and take a no-nonsense approach instead of trying to push issues under the carpet. Day and night, she told herself that she draws her boundaries and is capable of forgiving people who hurt her. It seemed pointless in the beginning, but she was pleasantly surprised with the state of mind she was getting into each passing day.

To decipher Linda's approach, we will need to identify the problem areas. One, it is more than a problem between Linda and her mother-in-law. It is part of a social malady that exists by default because of the power struggle involved. The mother-in-law thinks she must advise the young couple, and she does not realize she is intruding. She ignores the feelers because of this assumed authority. From Linda's perspective, she feels cornered because her mother-in-law is being obnoxious, and her husband's indifference contributes to the dilemma. Her helplessness also reflects a lack of skill in being able to prioritize her feelings, and this is the gap she needs to fill. Her upbringing reflects a tendency to put other people's feelings over herself, and when the other person is unfair, she feels trapped.

What would Linda's takeaway be from this experience? If the mother-in-law seems to be pushing the wrong buttons, it also means that there are parts within Linda that need healing. The first step is to overcome the victim mentality because it is, unfortunately, self-defeating. It will paralyze you in their presence, it will provoke you into being rude to them, and this will work to your disadvantage. But once you begin to see the ignorance and darkness surrounding the person, you will have your empathy and sense of humor in place to help you navigate the situation gracefully. It allows you to have fun and do your thing in place of spending precious energy wallowing in resentment and self-pity.

Let's Talk Money

I Embrace Difficult Situations to Bring Clarity

We are used to seeing social experiments establishing how women and money talk don't gel beyond a point. A lady who can talk about money and how to make money is a goddess of sorts you don't stumble upon in real life. Normalizing money talk in social conversations is so much more empowering.

Codie Sanchez is the contrarian we must fall in love with. Evolving into running a million-dollar media company and a handful of investment companies from starting as a talented journalist is a story that inspires. "I never much liked coloring inside the lines" is how she describes herself on her webpage (Sanchez, n.d.). She questioned the hardwiring in her to have this weird relationship with money which unlocked a new universe for her. Sanchez learned the rules of the game when she began to look at money differently. She discovered a new way of life and is now sharing her secrets with the world. To the reader, the question "What is it that will inspire me?" begged to be asked.

"I'm by no means the smartest, but I am perhaps the most willing to ask hard questions and then share my homework with other people willing to listen," says Codie Sanchez, who can leverage air to create a tornado. Her skills in leadership, risk-taking, and investments get people to fall off their chairs, but the most important message, even if one is not interested in making money, is that of overcoming self-limiting beliefs. Learn that, and life will get richer anyways.

Taking risks when one is looking to make wealth is the deal. Businesses would fail, and money could sink, but not giving up becomes possible when keeping your eye on your objective, even during the hard days. Visualizing your goals by keeping them in your range of eyesight is the way to carry them through. The moment we internalize that failing is often going to be part of the game, it stops intimidating us. It is the process of releasing the resistance to money. In the evolution of the human mind, money is a new entrant. We can safely say that the people who have an abundance of money and the people who struggle both have not completely understood its nature. People who make the same decisions can fall on the side of success or failure. It's just that the success part is spoken about, and the other is quick to be buried.

Until We Live In Denial

I Am Always Part of the Solution

"Not all the days of practicing affirmations are easy. Some days are a complete disaster because the mind will resist so much and drain every bit of energy out of you. We need to know that it is natural. Somedays are about letting it be and sitting through the pain in complete acceptance. A state of complete surrender of control is okay and not to be resisted. But come back the next day, and you will be surprised." said Brenda, recounting her challenging days.

When asked how she kept at it on days she did not feel like it, she said, "There were many days when things turned hopeless. But instead of giving up, my mind would tell me to try something different, like changing the sentence or something like that, and that was surprising. It was as if my brain now refused to give up," she elaborated.

In hindsight, she had ignored all the red flags, and today she couldn't forgive herself for that. It was a dizzy love story. She was 23 and had begun her career as a banker. A string of fantastic academic achievements and a dream paycheck had given her the confidence to make decisions on her own. Brenda met Samuel at the coffee shop on a sunny Saturday morning. His boyish grin as he cracked jokes with his six-year-old niece was enough to weaken her knees. She was sitting two tables away at the quaint cafe with her colleague and found herself staring at him more than she liked to admit. He had noticed. The next few months had Brenda in a different zone. The agonizing torment of love was so addictive that nothing else seemed to matter to her. Sam was a talented singer and working on building a career. His passionate love, his erratic schedules, the mavericks he hung around with, his non-conformist spirit, everything about him endeared her. It was as if they completed each other, and there was nothing more to seek. Two stable years of dating gave Brenda the confidence to think of marriage. Sam was not yet sure because his career options were very fluid at this stage, but Brenda was in no mood to listen since she was convinced that the marriage would give Sam the space and peace of mind to carve out a niche for himself. They loved the, as their friends put it, "creativity marrying stability" hue of their life.

In time the demands of other aspects of life began to present themselves in the marriage. Brenda's career was taking off superbly. Her job demanded time and energy but gave them financial stability. Sam's tendency to be lost in his lyrics, or travel alone on a whim, his neglected housework, and those unpredictable moods that made him irresistibly attractive in the first place began to gradually bother Brenda. She found it difficult to cope with the demands of the job and the house and tried to talk it out with Sam. Sam was unable to get her perspective and began resenting her behavior which he now found overbearing. For Brenda, the bills started mounting, and for Sam, his self-respect began to feel threatened.

For both Sam and Brenda, the shock of discovering that the love of their life was now causing them to hurt began to take its toll. Days were spent in nasty arguments or cold silences. Sam would go into a shell and not communicate for days. The silent treatment caused more damage than a showdown, and Brenda only felt pushed to the corner. It took her a while to realize that it was a tactic to silence her. He would refuse to engage in a conversation about anything she felt strongly about. The passive-aggressive behavior was the emotional abuse that Brenda was left to deal with. Her days were spent in hopelessness. All her achievements began to look not just inconsequential but working against her. In her state of conflict, sleep was disturbed, and she was always lost in thought. In desperation, she sought help. The interventions of a marriage counselor and therapist began on a painful note, with many wounds getting opened, but eventually helped them reconcile to each other's needs and limitations. Brenda chose objectivity and positivity despite all the trauma. She kept telling herself that things could be sorted out with some initiative and that everything was alright since they were ultimately two individuals needing respect and space—marriage, like all human relationships, required effort to make it work.

Voicing An Opinion Is the Nightmare

The Universe Takes a Step Toward Me Every Time I Take One Toward It

Bisha was known as someone with a large heart. Her friends loved her, and her colleagues respected her for her quiet dignity. But Bisha saw herself as an inadequate personality. She knew deep within her that she was capable of achieving much more in life and that she was far more talented than a lot of people who were in positions of influence around her. She envisioned herself to be a changemaker and fighter. She would feel embarrassed thinking about it, but she was convinced she had more talent than her top boss. But the trouble was she was clueless about the path to take. She would freeze every time she wanted to express her thoughts at a gathering. She was too polite to challenge an idea in public, and she was too empathetic to question the policy that was clearly not working. Even complimenting a colleague was impossible because she was afraid her opinion would be misunderstood. The contradiction of not being able to voice out an opinion when she wanted to was excruciatingly painful for Bisha. It was frustrating to see other people get accolades for things she would have done much better.

Her virtues of patience and having a cool head were working against her because her bosses had no clue that she was capable of being a leader and a go-getter. The despair was only increasing with the passing years. Having been stuck in a rut, Bisha turned to affirmations because she had heard a friend mention it in passing. She began to write her wishes down. It felt dubious, and she chided herself for her lack of self-respect. If only things were so simple, she would mutter in anger. But curiosity got the better of her. She thought it would be fun to do things that felt wrong. *Well, things that feel right do not seem to be working, let me do something truly new. I will go by faith since the idea of affirmations has been around for a long time.*

Ignoring the cringy feelings, she continued to write and say her affirmations daily. They were atrocious ones, feel-good ones, rebellious ones, and all sorts of statements. But she kept going. About four months into her secret indulgence, she found herself making a point in a meeting that stumped her. It was a polite but strong statement that people would not expect to be coming from Bisha. But it turned out that the top management took her viewpoint seriously and modified the marketing plan. The results spoke for itself, and she earned the respect of the organization. It was only the beginning of game changes for Bisha. She had started to believe and embody what she told herself. It did not matter if it felt true or not.

Manifesting My Dream Career

I Do My Best, and My Goal Is Not to Try and Beat Others

"Every day, I would let myself know why I couldn't be a writer. Oh, Rachel, there are such talented writers out there; you don't stand a chance. Who will pay the bills if I don't have a paying job? The economic burden of being a writer is tremendous. It is no longer a respected thing, going by the amount of garbage being published nowadays. I better spend my energy doing something more productive. These were the nature of the self-talk I would indulge in every time that tiny voice within me would beg to want to write. I had become adept at muffling it," laughed Rachel while narrating her story. "When the pandemic hit, and I lost my job, something shifted within me. It was not that I wouldn't find another job in the hospitality industry. I was good. But the forced pause gave that tiny voice a fresh lease on life. But my self-talk wouldn't give up either. This time, like a mother finally asking the older child to shut up so that the younger one would get a chance to explain, I let my tiny voice do the talking. When my internal dialogue changed, I found myself with forty articles on my blog and five publications to my name in one year. I got back to work after a sabbatical, but my writing continued at its own sweet pace. Never have I been a happier soul." Rachel said while speaking at a conference she was invited to as a speaker.

I radiate confidence and positivity. I am unstoppable in my journey to thrive. I thrive in all areas of my life.

Chapter Four:
AFFIRMATIONS FOR PERSONAL GROWTH

Let us delve into the tough affirmations women have used as a no-nonsense approach to manifesting the best life for themselves. Each success helped them unlock the next level of affirmation and boldly go where they have never been before. Go on, use them as your stepping stone to an exciting journey; the reward will entirely be your creation. The stories around the affirmation will help build it around the context of everyday situations, thus making it easy to apply in real life.

Maria Luisa Arroyo Cruzado, author and poet, says, "I vowed, now at 55, to ground and manifest my constellation of creative writing projects. Without asking permission. Without apology. Owning my brilliance" (Botton, 2023). If only many of us would be able to make such a style statement!

I Accept People Close to Me the Way They Are

Dolly's mind was reeling. She had just discovered that her husband's family was talking behind her back and passing unfair judgments about her. She was upset and tried talking about it to her husband. But to her utter shock and dismay, he refused to dialogue with her on this issue. Any attempt to open a conversation would end in nasty fights jeopardizing the otherwise healthy relationship with her husband. Dolly decided to work on it by accepting people's weaknesses instead of resisting and resenting their behavior. To her surprise, she found her solutions while functioning from this frame of mind.

I Can Understand Why Intimate Relationships Tend to Trigger the Most

Dolly now had the discernment to understand that she needed to approach the situation with consideration and patience. She needed to handle the complicated interpersonal dynamics in a fair yet firm manner. She needed to make it obvious that nobody — not even her otherwise loving husband — could bullshit around her and get away with it. She had to study the situation and assess it objectively without allowing her feelings to rule her actions.

I Can Correct My Habits That Get in the Way of Being a Positive Person

Dolly stopped being reactive or passive in many areas of her marriage. This she did without being dramatic, with small sure steps so that she was an active partner who would not take any kind of domination. She was actively setting her boundaries so that she had the moral high ground. Meanwhile, she began to slowly but surely build a healthy distance from her husband's family. She would be courteous when she met with them, but they got to feel her boundaries that were not to be crossed. By taking these little doable steps, she found herself not caring about what people spoke about her behind her back. She had essentially taken the wind out of their sails without lifting a finger. She had the right affirmations in her head all the time. She had told herself she was dignity personified.

I Have a Mindset That Is Open and Unbiased

Our mental health is getting challenged every day, more than we want to admit. We appear to manage somehow with spurs of releasing the tension by screaming at random people and during random times. And when things get intense, or there is built-up pain, it gets more serious than that. Professional help has to be sought without a doubt. Support from trusted people will come if we seek help. What if we had tools to help us navigate our lives? It would surely work in preventing us from reaching tipping points, provided we open our minds to new possibilities.

I Am Building the Skills Needed to Love Myself Because I Deserve to Be Seen and Respected

For some strange reason, negative affirmations are easier to test out than positive ones. Feeling ashamed of oneself comes easily, while forgiving seems like a tall order. A careless comment lodges itself in our mind easily, while a compliment is quickly forgotten. The plausible explanation is that threat is taken more seriously by our instinct than safety. But when there is no threat to life, we need to deploy our thinking brain to re-calibrate itself, and this is where positive affirmations come into the picture. We need to keep telling the primate part of our brain that the world is a safe place, and we need to move on.

I Am Unapologetic to People Who Like Putting Me Down

Can you recollect a time when someone believed in lies about you or passed judgments about your behavior without hearing your side of the story? It is tempting to barge in and give an explanation. But reflecting on it makes one realize that seeking validation from such people is pointless. They were, in any case, waiting for an excuse to point fingers at you. The behavior is thus a reflection of their insecurities and has nothing to do with your worth. Self-respect and self-love are like nurturing a tiny plant. It needs unconditional care and being surrounded by people who realize your value. So go on and have fun. Don't bother to justify; let them keep guessing!

I Am the Custodian of My Uniqueness

She was a software engineer with sharp business acumen. Twelve hours at the office was bliss for her, and she could be trusted to take on any challenge or risk that came her way. However, the story at home was a complete disaster. It was as if guilt was the basis of her identity. She functioned on the premise that she was not good enough as a wife and mother of two growing kids. Meera got her freedom the moment she realized that she is fine the way she is.

I Seize Every Opportunity of Self-Care

Being an Asian married to an Italian-American partner, Meera did have her set of challenges. She was treading on unfamiliar parenting patterns that had thrown her off track from the word go. Babies sleeping in a separate room was alien to her imagination, and she had immersed herself in work to overcome the conflicts that would crop up now and then. The adolescent kids were having a tough time relating to her now, and frustration was only growing in the family. A chance meeting with a life coach got Meera working on herself. For the first time in decades, she stopped looking at herself as a victim of circumstance. She realized she needed to take ownership, and for that, she had to love herself and recognize her strengths. When she began respecting her uniqueness, her family seemed to toe the same line. It was no short of a miracle for Meera. Today, her daughters see a champion in their mother.

I Find the World Changes as I Change My Thoughts

"When you think you are the hammer, everything in the world appears to be a nail," Professor Martha curtly remarked as Eva gave her the hundredth excuse for not submitting her thesis on time. Eva was losing confidence by the day. The influence of friends and ambitions to make it big on social media compromised her work ethic and values. She narrowly avoided being sucked into the vortex, but not before suffering scarring and losing confidence in all of her skills. She became a loner and would dwell on her thoughts all day. She would put off doing her homework and struggle to keep up academically. She started to convince herself that the world was not to be trusted and would find adequate justifications for her beliefs. When her roommate dragged Martha to the student counselor one fine day, Martha's life began to change. She was urged to alter her way of thinking, and she eventually started to see things differently. It was as if the world flipped when her thoughts changed.

I Proudly Discover a New Facet of Myself Every Single Day

Maya wasn't sure what kind of personality she wanted to see in herself. She was a beauty consultant in a new city in her early 30s, and she was handling herself bravely. But she made it plain that she did not want to turn out like her mother. Maya struggled to comprehend her mother's refusal to alter her perspective on anything. Her mother's opinion about people, travel, young people, fashion, food, and everything else under the sun was pretty much the same as 30 years earlier. With age, her world was only getting smaller. Though Maya enjoyed spending time with her mother, she found her predictability very annoying and difficult to engage in any meaningful conversation.

I Have No Limitations Except the Ones I Impose on Myself

The exasperation gave Maya a clear mission once she sat down to deliberate on it. She decided to work towards building a personality that would grow and expand with time. Unlike the norm, she did not want to go back to familiar paths to chart out her future. She would use the resources the present world had to offer. Her quest got her to understand some fundamental truths. One is that we spend the majority of time repeating the same thoughts we had the previous days, hence the same behaviors, choices, opinions, and experiences that repeat over and over, making them eventually automatic. We get enterprising in some superficial things, perhaps, but 99% of the things remain unchanged. She was super conscious of how she wanted to speak, behave, and change. From that point on, with affirmations as her guiding star, began a thrilling journey for Maya, and boy, did she surprise herself every other day.

Negative Emotions Only Serve as My Fuel to Become a Better Me

Cynthia would find herself boiling with rage every time her colleague would lavish praise to her face. Astra's hypocritical good mornings and cozying up annoyed her to no end. Well, because she was aware that this was the very person saying mean things behind her back. But civility did not allow Cynthia to make her rage known to Astra, and she had put up a fake smile despite seething inside. The trouble was that it affected Cynthia's peace of mind. She needed a practical way out of the situation. She knew she would get her peace of mind only by giving Astra a piece of her mind, but that was not an option, and she decided to channel the energies to her favor.

I Can See It When People Want to Hold Me Down With Them

The tendency to get consumed by rage or disgust does put us in danger of getting provoked. Cynthia had to channel that strong negative energy into something constructive. The energy load it created would otherwise become destructive, affecting her or someone else in the process. She found her peace by diverting this into her job and self-improvement. Without a confrontation, she showed Astra that she did not care for her opinions. It was Astra's turn to get frustrated because all her attempts at pulling Cynthia down were not working, and she had no choice but to keep her opinions to herself from then onwards.

I Exude Strength and Warmth

In Compelling People: The Hidden Qualities That Make Us Influential (Neffinger & Kohut, 2014), the essence of what makes someone an appealing personality was deconstructed. The arguments put forth succeeded in laying bare before us the qualities that contributed to making a person charming and influential. The formula was elegant, simple, and something that we all can work on if desired: The optimum combination of strength and warmth a person radiates determines a winning personality. Too much strength or too much warmth would upset the balance that is needed to be respected and liked. The moment we adopt the position that we have the skills needed to navigate through life, the strength appears to come from nowhere. When we realize that we are facilitators for all good things that can happen, the warmth also begins to radiate.

I Am Emotionally Secure, and Therefore People Feel Safe Around Me

When people are being mean and indifferent to others, it generally means they are hurt and inadequate themselves. People can only give what they have. If you are disturbed by negative emotion, that would also mean the presence of similar hurt within you. We get hurt when external negativity finds a match within us; otherwise, it would die off and would not affect us in the first place. It explains why a similar experience can invite very different reactions from two people. Taking bad experiences as a chance to check one's own emotional scorecard is a great idea. We would end up thanking the other person for bringing the rot hidden inside us to light as it allows us to work on it. You will find that positive energy radiating from you draws people of similar frequencies to you.

Tranquility Is My Default State of Mind

Quitting was a courageous step for Bushra. She had worked hard to get a job that was now draining her. She no longer found satisfaction in being a dental surgeon and wanted to be a full-time life coach, all to the shock of her parents, who had stood by her through the long, grilling years of training to be a professional. The turmoil in her mind was too much for her to bear. Retracing her steps would disappoint everyone who cared for her. She did not have the strength to carry through that in her present state of mind. If letting go meant she was a failure to the world, then to her, quitting meant freedom to live her life. She realized she had no other challenge other than to transcend her self-limiting thoughts. The opinion of others would have meaning only if her mind absorbed it. The moment she stopped soaking in what did not belong to her, she found tranquility. She has the strength to determine her destiny.

I Don't Get Caught up in Other People's Issues

This one is tricky, especially when the other is a close friend or a loved one. It gets counterintuitive because it makes you feel inhuman. It will appear to imply that one should not be helping when our dear ones are in trouble or are going through extremely challenging situations. Offering advice only when they specifically ask for it, letting them know that you are there to give them unconditional support, and letting them know that they are capable of fighting is the greatest gift one can give. Doing the firefighting for them can be a disservice. Your moral support will work best if they know that you will always give them an unbiased opinion. Sometimes, all they need is another perspective of the situation. Deciding what works is still in their area of autonomy.

I Know Why People Misbehave, and I Am Capable of Giving Them Opportunities to Come Out of Their Shackles

Getting her partner to discuss something about his behavior that was troubling her was like trying to nail jelly onto the wall. He would not be open to a conversation. Natalie's problem was that he made it difficult for her to give him honest feedback. His quick retorts that invalidated her opinions, his sarcastic comments, and his rude silence made her feel like she was in unsafe territory. Her bottled-up emotions led her to become angry, resentful, and bitter about many things in their marriage. She felt cornered and unable to do anything much about the passive-aggressive behavior. Their interactions would often swing between cold silences and aggressive flare-ups. Natalie had to stop being reactive and begin to look at the whole situation in a new light.

My Comfort Zones Are the Ones That Tell Me That It's Time to Take the Next Big Step

During a session with her counselor, Natalie had the realization that her partner's fear of criticism was the root of the issue. Every time she offered him feedback, he froze, and his aggression was a form of self-defense against this imagined threat. She came to the awareness that harboring resentments, though it felt comforting, was hurting both of them. She became mindful that she needed to understand the motivations behind his responses. It originated from a place of vulnerability rather than strength. She veered off course and started concentrating on his advantages. She also started to voice her ideas with confidence and took the initiative to keep the lines of communication open. Her confidence and quiet dignity rubbed off on him too. He gradually started to respect her viewpoints and open up. She had reworked the dynamics of their communication that stopped him from feeling intimidated. He was able to overcome his unwillingness to accept criticism because of the environment Natalie fostered.

I Can Decide How People Treat Me, and I Am a Badass Who Repels Manipulation

We are sometimes caught up with people we just can't stand. Their behavior gives you the shivers, and you want to run as far away from them as possible. But what if they happen to be your partner, in-laws, or even a parent? The emotional abuse can get unbearable, no doubt. You feel constantly invalidated, you are made to feel used and disrespected, and whatever you do or don't do would not change their attitude towards you. Turns out that it is a very relatable feeling with most people we meet.

If we have to deal with them, we need to have the diagnosis of their condition right. Otherwise, we would be in for a frustrating, never-ending struggle that would sap our energy perpetually. The fundamental truth is that people stuck in darkness cannot radiate light. They will only spread misery through their dealings with people around them. But there is another factor that succeeds in the negativity reaching you. You will absorb the darkness strongly only if there is a part of you that needs healing. It is like deadwood catching fire. When fire spreads, it is the dry leaves that lap them up readily, not the healthy ones. Once self-awareness comes in, you will find that the toxicity no longer affects you, and you can build healthy boundaries to protect your peace. People will continue to dig their graves; you need not bother proving them wrong. It is a complete waste of energy.

I Double-Down on My Strengths

"I learned that my strengths lie in advancing causes and the people I believe in. For me, this means helping others achieve their goals by bringing them together at retreats and events," Selena Soo (2023) writes on CNBC Make It.

Selena Soo has her hands on the pulse of the market. She advises entrepreneurs and influencers on their next best strategy, but why would they put their money on a self-proclaimed introvert? The contradiction is intriguing for sure. Soo makes her millions in a job that is networking-heavy. She is quick to point out the misconceptions introverts subject themselves to. She decided to rather spend her bucks on her strengths. Here, it did not really matter if she liked socializing because she liked helping. Her success stories and the gratitude people shower on her is what she taps into to repeat the success over and over.

I Can Smell Gas-Lighting From a Mile Away!

Nancy Drew was clueless. Unlike her famous namesake in the fictional world, she appeared to be the quintessential sitting duck. Her colleagues at work, her partner at home, and even her children knew she could easily be steamrolled into complying with their needs. She simply did not know assertiveness. Someone had to only draw a long face, and she would change her opinion to their favor. She dreaded rejection and was ready to pay any price to feel wanted. So what was the problem? Nancy's sense of self-worth dipped so low that she imploded with its pull. She quit her job and refused to get out of her room until the day she decided not to believe what others made her feel.

I Am a Style Icon Who Sets the Pace for People Around Me

On many occasions, we fail to realize that it is not necessary for us to like everyone who comes our way. Is there a surety that people will agree with us or even like our attitudes? Nope, and so be it. "What action do I need to take?" you may ask. Well, close your eyes and visualize the kind of person you would like to be. Observe the way she talks, walks, and dresses, the statements she makes, and the aura she exhibits. Open your eyes and write what you just saw, or draw animations, symbols, or whatever helps you jot down the personality. Now look at it every single day. You will see yourself morph!

I See That I Am Being Used as a Doormat—I Will Change It Now

She was expected to put up with and cover up the scars of her partner. Faiha did not resist because she had no idea she could. It was expected of any wife to empathize with the shortcomings of the husband and help him navigate life, so said her mother as parting advice on her wedding day. She did not realize that she was only becoming a safe house where his vices were getting parked. The need to heal and overcome was not there in him. That is when Faiha realized it was exhausting her, and she would continue to be the doormat if she remained passive. She made an effort to tell her husband in clear terms that he needed to get professional help in overcoming his mood swings. It initially shocked him, but it forced him to contemplate looking for a solution to his problems. Standing up for herself got Faiha much-needed peace of mind and strengthened their relationship in the long run.

I Am Grateful to Have You in My Life

Try using the name of the person who is troubling you to show gratitude, and you will be amazed to find the feeling of power you manifest over the situation. There is great empowerment in unconditional acceptance of how people turn out. It is not about giving in to their whims and fancies but accepting them without resistance at a spiritual level. Questioning why your boss is a heartless monster is a rejection of that person at the spiritual level. This resistance makes us weak, and we respond from a lower frequency level of anger, disgust, pity, or sadness. Try taking a contrary stand and accept that the other person is at their place in evolution, perhaps having a long way to go. You will suddenly find yourself functioning at a higher level of frequency where there is compassion and empathy.

I Am Too Self-Aware to Be Imbibing Other People's Toxicity

Sometimes we take in the toxic behaviors of the people in our lives and start behaving just like them. The energy of the place seems to affect our attitudes too. It takes a certain maturity to recognize and deal with it, but it is not rocket science either.

"If you want something to come in, you must learn to let go," her dad used to say often. Elina felt stuck in a difficult marriage. She was the square peg that her husband was trying to hammer into a round hole. She was walking on eggshells every day, constantly watching out for one explosion or the other. Nothing seemed to be working to calm her down until she mustered the courage to seek help. The affirmation practices made her nervous. She would break down and appear to have become more vulnerable than before. But her mentor asked her to go through those seemingly helpless motions with complete surrender. She was encouraged to release the resistance. She gradually learned to separate herself from her emotions to be able to look at things objectively. From that detached position, she was able to see the obstacles that were preventing her from navigating her difficult partner. She took the first step of finding a simple job to keep her out of the house and build up her savings. The liberation put her into a better frame of mind that, in turn, helped her make sensible decisions.

People Who Steamroll Me Lose Me

Jasmine survived her childhood with her ability to suppress her emotions and maintain a stoic stance every time her parents fought. But this repression of feelings began to backfire when she got married. Her inability to recognize and express her needs put her in a position of disadvantage in her new family setup. She would not say it if she did not agree with her partner's opinion. People took it that she was okay with everything they did or said while her thoughts remained bottled inside her.

It is important for us to be able to see our emotions with clarity. We need to face our demons if we have to and not live in denial if our emotions have to work for us and not against us. Jasmine's realization led her to become an active partner whose opinions mattered in the family. She took tiny steps and trained herself to be able to express her emotions healthily.

I Create My Reality, and Nobody Else Decides My Fate

"Saying my affirmations aloud was important for me, and it always went along with journaling and daily breathwork rituals. The combinations felt right and helped in converting my wishes to reality," recollected Dahlia during her talk at the school she was invited to as a special guest. For Dahlia, working with numbers gave her happiness. Her otherwise eventless life came alive when she sat down with her favorite subject. The malice and bias of society, the thoughtless, racist, sexist attitudes of people that surrounded her, all vanished into thin air in the fair and beautiful world of mathematics. As she grew, she began to see her purpose in teaching children and sharing knowledge that would help other young souls navigate the world.

My Fears and Worries Are Rungs of the Ladder That I Climb Toward My Glory

Dahlia's first shocker came when she was rejected after an interview with a prestigious school in her town. Though they did not voice it, it was clear that they were uncomfortable with her tendency to stutter. They were worried about putting off the parents and the impact on their brand value. That they were losing out on a prodigal math teacher did not even occur to them and did not seem to matter. After all, there were so many other good candidates to choose from.

I Succeed Because I Dwell On My Strengths

Dahlia could not imagine applying for a job as a teacher again because the outcome seemed all too obvious. She only saw failure ahead of her, and this made her anxious. But she couldn't imagine doing anything else either. She had no moral support, no backup, or entitlement either. Her confidence went to an all-time low, and the possibility of getting into clinical depression was looming large. Her friends could see it coming and could only helplessly watch. But something in her desperately wanted to not lose hope. She stumbled upon a podcast of affirmations and got curious. Her logical mind saw the merit of channeling her energy into getting a desired outcome, so much like applying a formula during number crunching. Her fertile mind caught on to the practice like a fish takes to water. A few months into persistent practice got her completely zoned into her talent at teaching. She began by teaching neighborhood kids and ventured into making simple YouTube videos. She had decided not to care about her stutter.

My Success Expands in Proportion to the Size of My Dreams

Before Dahlia made her first video, she had already visualized a hundred of them in her mind. It was as if they already existed, and she had to just download them from her mind and upload them on YouTube. The initial terrors vanished quicker than anticipated, and she began reeling out content. She resisted the need to be perfect. Good was good enough at that stage because it was more important to act. Her work began to speak for itself when people began to see the brilliance in her teaching. They didn't seem to notice the stutter, though it was very much there. Schools began approaching her with teaching assignments, which she did not need now. Dahlia now functions on her terms and took off like greased lightning, with people watching helplessly, only this time, in awe.

I Think Far Beyond My Present Circumstances, and I Leapfrog on Time Because I'm Prepared

We miss the idea that we become byproducts of the energy we inhabit. From the word go, stereotypes about our race, sex, and other social characteristics influence the narrative we tell about ourselves. It simply does not occur to us that we are building patterns of thinking and reacting based on our immediate environment. It does not necessarily follow that something is true just because it has existed forever, but we somehow ignore this as we navigate our days, blissfully unaware of our low self-esteem, shaky confidence, and self-constricting attitudes. And when opportunities to up the ante present themselves before us, we either fail to recognize it or we are not prepared to own it and end up stuck.

I am full of energy and ready to tackle the day.

My body is capable of increadible things.

I believe in the woman I am becoming.

Chapter Five:
AFFIRMATIONS FOR
OVERCOMING CHALLENGES

We have layers of rejection, shame, emotional abuse, and guilt ingrained in us that determine our choices in life and play out in our present relationships. Let us stop denying that we all have dead wood inside of us that burns too easily. Would it help if you dare begin to think uniquely so that life starts to treat you differently? It's not easy because we have been told that the known devil is better than an unknown angel. It has been drilled into our subconscious that the herd mentality is safe. Stepping out of the line will invite immediate and brutal responses from the crowd and the whispers within. Change can very well begin with us. What if we become the torch bearer for ourselves and those who we would inspire?

Popular culture, strangely, has no interest in letting an individual know that they are good people who are capable of taking care of themselves. It has a strong vested interest in instilling self-doubt and the need for validation from others. But then why, you would ask. Biology has a good explanation for this. It is the survival of the fittest theory that gets us to adopt safe practices. For example, an individual's right to smoke will be overrun by society's interest to preserve health. Perfectly understandable. But the trouble is we use them as blanket principles to interfere with an individual's autonomy. Generally, women have it tough because of the patriarchal hue of society, although it is true that men are victims too. A woman's instinct to be nurturing and accommodating works against her more often than not. Curiously, her strength is taken as her weakness, and the woman is made to believe in the false narrative. Men and women have to be tough as far as protecting their peace is concerned. It ought to be a fair game!

I Am a Positive Rebel

Identifying problems can be challenging by themselves and need perseverance. No one can go far with a feeling of inadequacy deep down. Like bad driving skills, they will show up only when there is a crash. Anger, confusion, and a feeling of being constantly overwhelmed become our companions. Sometimes, to deal with all the disappointments, we end up creating such tough boundaries around us that the very boundaries prevent us from being ourselves. You would probably agree that it is a lousy deal as well. The good news is that we snap out of the bad bargains the moment we figure it out. Things begin to fall into place when we begin to know our strengths and begin to disrupt the patterns.

I Am Known to Be an Assertive Person Who Does Not Mince Words

By resetting our pre-existing belief systems in our minds, affirmations help us internalize fresh thinking. It is comparable to formatting a laptop that has irrelevant or defective software. The new beliefs are meant to anchor us and prevent us from crumbling and getting crippled by the lashes given by life. It is the empowering act of saying yes to the right approach that elevates us and thereby rejects self-defeating thoughts that push us further into the pit. Affirmations that have stood the test of time are those that have ultimately worked, no matter how complex or unique the issue. They are what help protect one's peace and navigate through mean, selfish, small-minded people and events that shake our very core. We don't want to waste our time and energy suffering other people's mentalities, nor be paralyzed by resentment and disgust that put us in trouble.

Shifting our minds to winning positions is a smart strategy. We need to master them and breeze through difficulties. If you find it unbearable to live with compromises, being the doormat, or at the receiving end of unfairness, adopt razor-sharp affirmations. They cut through the clutter and save you time. It will improve the quality of your life and make you feel proud of yourself whenever you look at yourself in the mirror. Be assertive and not aggressive.

I Am Super Responsive to Change

The best news we have heard in recent times is that the brain is very much capable of being rewired. The growth mindset phenomenon has given hope to all who have been living life reconciling to the fact that perhaps their intelligence and personality are determined by genes and other factors beyond their control and that nothing much was in their hands to do anything about it. Turns out that it is not true. Even if the purpose behind the practice of affirmations sounds convincing, we would need it to be backed by evidence. Since it is an intangible process, it was very easy to dismiss it as a pseudo-practice. It would not fit the bill as far as empirical evidence was concerned. Thankfully, neurological and physiological research tools have become more sophisticated than ever before, making it possible to prove associations better. You would agree that we can respond to situations that determine our success more than anything else.

My Physical Being Reflects My Will to Be a New Personality

Notice your body language change from defensive to oozing confidence in a winning situation. A study established that self-affirmation activates brain systems associated with self-related processing and reward and is reinforced by future orientation (Cascio et al., 2016). It is relevant to note that the study showed how people who practiced affirmations were successful in resisting threats to their competence and self-worth. They are motivated in comparison, and they were able to successfully change sedentary behavior because of an increase in activity in the brain's self-processing and valuation systems. In simple terms, they become more self-aware. Isn't it great news that solutions can come from within us? We just need to build the skills to extract them. Reinforcement is needed to maintain the activity, and even that gets better because the resistance gets lesser with every practice session. Research shows anecdotes of how interventions through affirmation have benefitted in dealing with stress, increased well-being, improved academic performance, and made people more open to behavior change. It improves the practitioner's ability to broaden one's perspective and reduce the effect of negative emotions, thus protecting overall psychological well-being (Cohen & Sherman, 2014).

My Lifestyle Follows My Intentions

The oriental lands have worked around the concept of the energy body for centuries now. It is an intelligence recognizing the power of the human body to channel energy to manifest its needs. Energy healing practices like Reiki and Pranic Healing are used to manifest the highest intentions by tapping the universal life force to accelerate what is rightly desired. It is used to heal physical and mental ailments and to manifest higher purposes. For instance, the yogic process manifestation has been laid down in the spiritual texts of India. The *Hanuman Chalisa* is an Indic compilation of 40 lines that is repeated for 40 days with a single-minded focus on manifesting anything. The basis is that affirmations made continuously for a fixed number of days create memory and repatterns the neurological pathways, thus leading the individual to align their physical, mental, emotional, and spiritual energy to the desired cause. This will ensure that all actions and choices lead them to the desired goal instead of moving around scattering their energies in a hundred different directions with no purpose. One may not see the results instantly, but it is sure to manifest in the due cycle of time. Specific breathwork and meditation techniques learned under guidance will accelerate the process so that one does not fall by the wayside in the endeavor of leading a meaningful life.

I Have the Emotional Tools to Handle Everything That Comes My Way

Let's face it: We cannot assume that just because we are aware of something that we will take action. In his book, *The Psychology of Money*, Morgan Housel (2020) makes a brilliant case of how behavioral skills play the most important role in people's decisions on money. "A genius who loses control of their emotions can be a financial disaster. The opposite is also true. Ordinary folks with no financial education can be wealthy if they have a handful of behavioral skills that have nothing to do with formal measures of intelligence," he rightly observes. The same would go for managing life as well.

I Think It Is Healthy to Upset the Apple Cart When Necessary

There is that nagging feeling of being on unsafe grounds that comes to us every once in a while when things appear to be going fine. When you are being silenced with love, when your thoughts are trivialized by a dominating partner or colleague, when your upbringing is not allowing you to push back when you get manipulated into something, or when others cross your boundaries are but some instances where you find yourself feeling the need to upset the apple cart. It is perfectly fine and, in fact, called for to protect your peace.

I Have the Conviction to Be Upfront With People Who Matter to My Peace

Tracy was having a tough time dealing with her manager. She was part of a three-member team reporting to Natalie. Natalie was efficient and hardworking and naturally expected high standards from her team members. That was fair in Tracy's view. But the trouble was that Natalie's way of giving feedback was aggressive and hurtful. Tracy was not the one to take it lying down. She fixed an appointment with Natalie to have a conversation on this. She was polite but gave clear feedback that Natalie's communication style was hurtful. This surprised Natalie but then led her to reflect on it, ultimately helping her and the office. The candor also won Tracy a newfound respect in Natalie's eyes, leading to a lifelong friendship between the two.

I Am Forthright, and Those Around Me Are Well Aware of It

Separating the person from the behavior is a skill that needs to be honed if you want to avoid falling on your face while trying to deal with jackasses. Let's face it: There have been times when we get into a difficult conversation with people who have been a pain in the neck, only to come out of it feeling that things have got messed up further. They do not seem to have got what you are getting to, and they point fingers at your behavior. This makes us less confident in our ability to deal with difficult people, and our resentment toward them increases. This resentment and disgust we have in our minds only increase our chances of messing up the relationship further.

Valuable Lessons Are Hidden in Unpleasant Situations, and I Learn From Them

This usually happens because our emotions take over the conversation, and our rational brain kind of shuts down. We lose control, and the other party succeeds in getting hold of ropes they can tie you up with. The dialogue turns into a messed-up power struggle, and we lose track of the core issue. Every time Sahiba brought up instances of her sister-in-law's manipulative behavior with her husband, her otherwise reasonable husband would end up losing his temper and get defensive. He would resist the conversation in the first place with reasons like, "No point talking about it; she is immature." But this did not help Sahiba because the unacceptable behavior continued. She realized that her husband was only closing doors for future conversations on this topic. She realized that she would get overcome by emotions whenever she spoke about her sister-in-law. She would speak in anger and disgust when she spoke. This emotion was picked up by her husband, and he felt she was belittling his family. He would then close his mind on what Sahiba was trying to convey, thus messing it up further for her.

I Build Healthy Coping Strategies

Sahiba decided to change course. She had to learn to separate the person from the behavior. She also had to keep her emotions under control. She had to learn to calmly communicate her point without seeming to venture into personal attacks on her husband's family. For starters, she confided her problems with a person whom her husband would be receptive to and got that person to talk to. The next time she had to have a difficult conversation with her husband, she was better prepared. She was able to keep her dignity and firmness while neatly carving out the issues and without appearing to slander the person as such.

She needed to work on not being misunderstood. That required her to be prepared for the other person blowing their top and wait calmly for their emotion to tide out. Her calmness would take the wind out of the other side and force them to talk rationally. This would also give her husband a chance to explain the background behind the behavior and show his empathy for Sahiba. Even if he could not anticipate the adverse consequences of his sister's manipulations in the future, he would be receptive to future conversations when the need arose. In certain situations, it would be possible for both of them to agree to disagree. For instance, Sahiba would not want to frequently meet up with her sister-in-law, and this would be respected by her husband. Unfair behavior is difficult to put up with. The anger and hurt tempt us to get even, or we freeze with resentment and disgust.

My Well-Being Comes From Inside of Me and Is Independent of Outside Validations

She would find herself nodding to everything, from where they should be holidaying, what they should be spending on, what they should be eating. Everything from trivial to substantial decisions was presented to her, backed with such forceful explanations that there was no way of not agreeing to them. Sylvia was the passive partner in the relationship. She was, however, not passive at work or looking back, either as a student or as a daughter. She could see the contradiction but did nothing about it for fear of confrontation. The equation continued to intrigue her, and Sylvia began to look closely at the dynamics of her marriage with Andre. She needed to define her self-worth in clear words to progress.

My Communications Reflect Receptiveness and Empathy

One fine day, the puzzle fell into place. They were at the departmental store choosing a gift for the neighbor's child. Whenever she would pick something, he would not have an opinion on it, but whenever he chose something, he would influence her to agree to his choice. His choice of gift was purchased. She realized that while she would accommodate Andre's viewpoints on things, he would not do the same with her ideas. Her views would be met with silence, and the balance would tilt in his favor. The joy ride to change began for Sylvia from then on. She would pause and deliberate before agreeing with Andre. She would also put forth her view with equal conviction, nudging Andre to treat both opinions with equal weight, and life changed for Sylvia since.

I Am Enough to Take on the System

She was a thorn in the flesh, and they wanted her out at the earliest. Polonia had earned her place as the head of school on her merit. The top management changed five years into her position, and it was a disaster for Polonia from then on. They found her ways too idealistic to fit into the competitive academic structure of the schools in the city. They had no patience to see her "curriculum experiments," as they called it. She had won the heart of the students who found her to be empathic and humane; they were all too ready to listen to her. But the teachers thought she was a pain in the neck. Her questioning of their tried and tested teaching methods irked many of them. Very few teachers related to her spirit and were ready to take on the change.

Every Discomfort Kick-Starts Greater Progress in My Journey

Polonia was being steamrolled at different levels. But she was not the one to chicken out. Every time they pointed fingers, she showed them the mirror by establishing how alternative paradigms in education were making their mark in the world. She showed how redundant methods were causing havoc in the minds of the learners. She had her data, she used the support of the latest developments in pedagogy, and she told them in plain words that she wouldn't be cowed down. This disarmed her opponents systematically because they found it difficult to counter her stand. It would have been very easy for them to unsettle her if she was not confident of the path she was taking or if there had been compromises in her work. She was able to tap into the voice of progressive parents who came forward to express their solidarity. She won her respect despite powerful people standing in her way.

I Accommodate Difficult Emotions in Order to Plan the Overcoming Part

Greta had worked her way to get into her dream company. She was a corporate lawyer in her late 20s, raised in a home where honesty and ethics in the workplace were valued highly. She was confident of her abilities to do well in her career and aspired to a decent lifestyle to make her parents proud. After five years of interning in a mid-size law firm where she put her nose to the grind, she got her lucky break. Her dream was to work at Cod's, Manhattan's most sought-after Law Chambers. An opening came up, and before she knew it, she was in! She was on cloud nine, in awe of the legal luminaries at the office, and was so eager to learn. She was to report to Patricia, a savvy, sharp lawyer in her mid-thirties. She instantly caught Greta's imagination. "I want to be her," she said to herself. Three months into the job, Greta was an emotional wreck. She was filled with disgust, had self-doubts, and was completely disillusioned. Patricia was her nightmare! Greta felt emotionally abused by her boss's condescending and manipulative behavior. Much as she tried, she was clueless as to a way out of this tricky situation. She found herself dragging herself to the office every day. Quitting did not look like an option because that would break her self-esteem even further. The more she thought about it, the more she choked.

I Have Complete Ownership Over My Days Because I Know I Intentionally Earn Each One of Them

Greta confided in her friend, who suggested she meet a good therapist. This initiative helped her gain perspective. She was able to objectively look at the situation and see the faults of her boss without feeling overwhelmed. She was also able to see the responses that came from herself to the situation. Her inbuilt values could not tolerate a lack of integrity in others. In other words, her strengths were becoming her weaknesses. Now that she was equipped with the correct information, she needed the tools to help her navigate her days with Patricia. The self-affirmations she needed to have right now were crucial. It required her to now train herself to thrive in difficult situations without getting stressed. She would have to be tactful and assertive, and for that, she would have to change herself. Changing another person is not a choice. More important, it entailed finding ways of standing up to the bad behavior of her boss. As a consequence, it slowly dawned on Patricia that Greta could not be steamrolled. Since Greta never lost control of her emotions, there was no way Patricia could point fingers at her or use things to her advantage.

No One Can Make Me Feel Inferior Without My Consent

Alice wanted to be a teacher all her life, and she knew she had it in her to be a great one. She was academically brilliant, and acing the performance assessments was no big deal. Her strong interpersonal skills and pleasant demeanor garnered the respect of the top management of her dream school. All was well until the pressures of dealing with the profession began to take a toll on her. Situations were never ideal. Students misbehaved, parents were aggressive, colleagues shirked work, the salary did not match the service, and the curriculum was compromised to suit the level of the average student and jack up results. Alice also got sensitive to the fact that her profession was not well respected by a lot of people around her. She realized that her lifelong dream and desire to be an extraordinary teacher was not giving her the fuel to sustain herself. Something more would be needed to help her survive and overcome the challenges. She knew her work could influence lives for the better, but the hurdles were overwhelming and threatening to break her spirit.

I Do Not Verbally Confront Difficult People and Maintain a Dignified Firmness

Nothing can be more annoying to bear than being the subject of backbiting. Imagine realizing that people are not discussing issues with you but talking about you behind your back. It puts you in a position where you cannot clarify your stand because no one is asking for it in the first place; they are only judging and labeling. There is nothing much that can be done about it. Ignoring it is the most logical thing to do. But sometimes, this becomes tricky. Lucia found it difficult to ignore the fact that two of her colleagues were talking behind her back. She was lost on how she would bring it up with them, and it was also not possible to engage with them normally with this knowledge. Lucia's dilemma was that she was afraid she would lose her cool with them, which would only give them more fodder for slander. She did not want to be unfair like them either. Giving them the silent treatment was not her way of getting back. Confiding in her best friend also did not help much because they did not want to rock the boat either. She would cringe at the unfairness and struggle to take the right stand for a long time. After days and months of feeling miserable in her heart, the realization hit her one day.

My Creative Problem-Solving Abilities Land Me Golden Opportunities

Her affirmation of being a dignified person suddenly bore fruit. The answer was in letting go of the pain. She only had to let them dig their own grave. Time would tell the world in any case, and she did not have to initiate anything to clarify her position. She had to take this experience as an opportunity to refresh her goals of becoming a better human being. In fact, that adversity was to provide her with the manure for self-improvement. Her dignified silence serves as the biggest blow to her adversaries. Their malice was not getting the required oxygen to thrive because any slip on Lucia's part, where she lost control of her emotions, would have only given more wings to their petty behavior. Her silence was a big blow to them, and they had no choice but to give up. Most importantly, they did not realize that they had lost her respect and trust forever. The message was loud and clear. That they would miss out on Lucia's friendship and empathy because they didn't deserve her.

I Will Not Give Up Until I Learn to Stand Up for Myself

The most difficult of situations to deal with is when the behavior of people is unfair, and you are left to suffer it silently. The actions make us angry and hurt, but we are left clueless as to the best way of addressing it. Most often than not, the other person will not understand your detachment towards them and will use your silence against you. Talking it out will be met with immediate resistance and defensiveness. On the other hand, the conversation will turn in a way that you are busy explaining your actions.

I Listen to and Observe People With Benevolent Intentions

It's crucial in this circumstance to distinguish between their behavior and who they truly are. This will help you in keeping your responses reasonable at all points. Getting provoked into anger can make you seem to be an unreasonable person. When you think of them as someone who is dear to you and who, once in a while, acts funny, it becomes easy to get the upper hand. You are detaching yourself from the person, and this will help replace your hurt with true kindness. And as they say, no revenge is the best revenge. Don't get me wrong here; I am not for once asking you to gulp the pain. If you have to get a firm message across, do so by all means. But not by becoming emotional yourself and falling into their manipulative trap. Maintaining a distance and your dignified silence will be loud enough.

Sorry Dear, but I Cannot Be Manipulated Into Silence

You could use humor or decide to talk straight. Take your pick. But learn to recognize emotional abuse when it happens and address it proactively. Domestic violence is part of many intimate relationships, and most of the time, the victim is not even aware that it is abuse. This happens because the abuse is very subtle and cannot be boxed into a particular definition. It is a pattern if you care to notice because we go into denial mode whenever it happens. Maybe I heard it wrong, maybe I am misunderstanding, and I need to change so that they do not point out my weaknesses. These are the thoughts that run through the victim's mind whenever there is an instance of emotional abuse. You will only run the risk of being labeled crazy whenever you attempt to call it out. The abuser, who happens to be your otherwise loving partner, will cover it up using varied and cunning ways. Distraction is one such path. Another way is to cover it up with a lot of love and affection. Nobody would want to own up to their mistakes. Recognizing this intent also helps you keep your calm and prevents falling into the trap of getting even. Counter-manipulation or being mean in another situation is not going to help at all. This will only make you feel miserable and worsen the situation for both.

I Evaluate My Beliefs and Judgments Objectively

Lisa was made to feel bad about calling out her husband's nasty habit of making fun of her in public. Even her mother said she was being overindulgent and ungrateful. "How could you forget all the good things about the marriage, dear?" She would point out gently, and Lisa would instantly feel guilty and ashamed that she was being small-minded. The matter would rest until she would be shocked by the subsequent abuse. She would then respond by convincing herself that she was overreacting, or worse, that she deserved to be treated that way. Emotional abuse followed by silencing the woman is normalized in many communities, even in the most educated and advanced of them, and therefore putting up a resistance becomes challenging and spirit-breaking. The tiresome process of moving against the tide gets a lot of people to give up and compromise. A trade-off will find supporters, but fightback will be discouraged by one and all. It will most surely isolate you. The first step, therefore, is to be prepared for isolation, ruffling feathers, and name-calling. Because once you can truly transcend that part, it becomes liberating. What's more, Stockholm syndrome appears to be taking over. It is where the victim begins to sympathize with the abuser and begins to look for opportunities to support the abuser. This seems to happen a lot in the context of intimate relationships.

There Is No Other Word for It — It Is Abuse, Period

Many times, abuse gets disqualified as abuse, even in the victim's mind. If someone hits me, I can say I was hit with conviction, even if there is no evidence to show. But unfair behavior is near impossible to define because of its slippery, slimy nature. I would start doubting its validity as I speak about it. We will look around for examples of women who are worse off and are still coping bravely with an abusive partner for the sake of children, financial security, or whatever. We will talk ourselves into a trade-off and get into familiar territory once again. Dangerously, it feels normal and, therefore, acceptable.

Maria knew that emotional abuse was more traumatizing than physical abuse, but she did not see a way out of the maze. Because the trauma was hidden, no one, even she, could not see it or be part of the healing process. The result was that even in her mind, she would vehemently resist labeling her ordeal as emotional abuse. She preferred to stay silent and distract herself with other things that "mattered."

I Reject the "It's Got to Be You" Narrative That Society Tells Me

It hurts even worse when the person you are confiding in says, "But there are always two sides to the story." The intention, though noble, only succeeds in invalidating the feelings of the victim. It may, at the moment, cut the pain but force them to think of another way of looking at things, but in the long run, the abuse gets covered by a lot of ifs and buts. Another common comment when someone is trying to talk out their pain is, "What did you do to cause them to say that?" Even the most progressive of us seem to buy the popular narrative of shame and guilt every single time. We take the abuse, internalize it, and use the popular narrative to get into further self-inflicted emotional abuse. There is work to do, lots of it. The pushback will not tire you when you already believe that you are fine the way you are.

People Are in Awe of My Resilience

It was 2 a.m. and pitch dark. Jade heard her four-year-old daughter moaning in the bed next door. She went over to soothe her. The crying intensified, and to her shock, the child collapsed into her arms with eyes locked upwards. It was just the two of them since her husband was traveling for work. All Jade could do was put the child in the back seat of the car and drive to the closest hospital. She managed to reach the Emergency Room and caught her first breath only when the medics took over. By sunrise, they had stabilized the child and identified the seizure. The next few years had the household turned upside down, with the young couple doing everything to focus on their daughter's health.

Situations like this are not unusual in today's nuclear families. The untold stories of resilience and sacrifice required day in and day out by ordinary people to stay on track are no less consequential than war stories, so to speak. Tough times show us our capabilities. It is heartening to know that we are tougher than we believe we are. Sustaining that toughness needs to be handled smartly so that it leaves us with energy for all essential aspects of our lives.

I Am Antifragile

In his book, *Antifragile*, Nassim Nicholas Taleb (2012) defines antifragility as the quality of becoming stronger when exposed to stressors and risk. Notice that it is different from the quality of just being strong. When I am a strong person, my strength will be put to the test time and again with adversities. My ability to resist uncertainties is my measure of strength. But if I am antifragile, the adversities are the food with which I continue to gain strength. Every problem will be accepted gladly because that is the source of additional strength for me. How about living a life where I do not stay the same by resisting bad happenings but get better with each stressor? We do that when we have an open mind and the humility to accept that we are not always in control. Whether it is the mid-life crisis hitting or continued disappointments in life, we make them ours to give us the conviction to move on.

I Acknowledge My Limitations When Taking Stock of My Achievements and Failures

Claude Steel articulated a very fundamental need in every human in his theory of self-affirmation (Steele, 1988). He established that every time our self-image is threatened, whether by others or even ourselves, the motivation to gather back our scattered self-image arises in each of us. For instance, if I am criticized for shabby behavior, I must assure myself that I am not bad after all. There could be another instance where we fail to complete work on time because we have been too distracted by social media. We feel threatened by ourselves because we like to believe we are hard-working, but our actions are not consistent with our thoughts. Here also, we will then look for ways to assure ourselves that we are worthy of our respect. The point is that somehow we figure out a way to restore our self-esteem, even though we would have failed in the specific areas we are discussing.

My Time Is My Property and Does Not Get Taken Away Without My Permission

Assertiveness in self-care does not come easily to us. Time management skills kick in only with the ability to not leave too many loose ends. When there is no commitment, distractions fill up the space easily. Rose learned it the hard way when she had a shoddy research paper to submit after accommodating her family's perpetual requests to lend a hand in everything big and small.

I Am an Active Partner in My Marriage

When Kyra's husband insisted she handle the household finances without his help, she was forced to confront her insecurities. She reflected on her tendencies and came to terms with the fact that it was a self-sabotaging trait she had inherited. Once she diagnosed the root cause, she was able to open up to unlearning and relearning without feeling ashamed of herself. Every time she felt overwhelmed and made a mistake, she reminded herself of the complex litigation she had handled while telling herself I have got this; it's the tiny drops that make the ocean. She used to be terrified of discussing money, but she has since made a conscious effort to get through the mental wall. Once the mental obstacles were removed, she set to work sincerely on learning the fundamentals of finances, and in a matter of months, she was transacting like a pro. There was no turning around!

I Am Aware That There Is No Growth in the Comfort Zone and No Comfort in the Growth Zone

Woefully, the imposter syndrome hits the best of us, be it young children, adolescents, and adults. And it happens more often than we realize. The victims walk through life with a "what if I am found out" feeling constantly clouding their minds. It is a state of mind we get into at some time or the other where we are convinced that we tricked our way into achieving whatever we have, and it is only a matter of time before people find out we were no good. It is a powerful whirlpool that can suck us down. Specifically, crafting affirmations to remove self-doubt will help one crack the code and finally feel freedom.

I've Got This—I Make Tiny Moves Every Day That Build up Exponentially

Kyra was a mess when it came to understanding finances. She was a talented lawyer and thoroughly enjoyed her identity as an awe-inspiring professional. She was a charismatic personality with a big fan following. But her deft mind seemed to blank out every time she had to plan out her savings, assess her earnings, and decide on expenditures. She would simply give up and expect her husband to manage it for her. Turns out she grew up in a household where money was always a sticky point. Her father held on to every penny and would not spend on anything he thought was an excess. Every aspect of life, be it family visits or socializing, holidaying, education, or even something as trivial as buying ice cream on impulse, was based on how much money was getting spent. He was paranoid, but that's not how she perceived it as a child. She only knew that all decisions were to be made based on money, and therefore a lot of her unhappiness was associated with money. Her father's paranoia, in turn, came from his childhood trauma of seeing no food on the table one fine day. So it was a generational curse, and the self-limiting belief was manifesting in different ways with each of them.

Chapter Six:
AFFIRMATIONS FOR SPIRITUAL GROWTH

eeft̸ft̸ɓee

"When I was clever, I wished to change the world, when I am wise, I wish to change myself," goes a quote by the great poet-philosopher Rumi (A Quote by Rumi, n.d.). Each one of us is complete in ourselves, but we end up projecting our needs onto people around us. The uncontrollable need to change others has spoiled many relationships; it continues to eat into our quality of life and keeps us in its clutches. The more intimate the relationship, the greater the expectation. We want our partners, family, and friends to behave in certain ways and change their attitudes so that they align with us. We feel incomplete when the other person does not toe the line, and we feel it's okay to push our expectations down their throats. Making time for spiritual growth in this world of external validations can be a challenge, especially when there is no immediate incentive, and there is so much to achieve. Collective wisdom gained over thousands of years has established that looking inward is the answer.

I Know It's Time to Look Within Me When I Encounter Pain and Struggles

The point is that if a random statement from outside of us can spiral us out of our control, deliberately tapping into good things from inside of us will serve us well. The nervous system responds to stimuli, either negative or positive. The choice of whether to allow negative triggers to take over or to counter them with helpful material is a choice. Exercising this choice, however, needs repetition, cajoling, and patient training, much like the elephant. Writing down your affirmations daily does exactly that. The rider's theoretical knowledge will not help; the elephant needs training every single day (with rest days allowed!). If Sara could have replaced her feeling of helplessness at her husband's narcissistic tendencies by playing on her strengths of building appropriate response systems, her precious energy would serve her well in handling the issue.

My Attitude Determines Whether a Situation Is a Threat or an Opportunity

"If you want something, say it out loud," Zyra's kindergarten teacher had told her lovingly five decades ago. Something about it stuck with her for life. Whenever she got nervous about asking or voicing out her needs, that voice would go booming in her heart. We don't always ask. We are too overwhelmed, too proud, too afraid, too impatient to just ask. We resist forming that sentence and speaking, whether it is to people, to organizations, or to the universe. When we make an effort to speak out, we are very likely to get a response. We love to decide and think on behalf of the other person, and we don't ask because we think we know what the answer is going to be. What we want from life will remain a notion until we dare to say it out loud. Let's use our voices to bring our dreams alive.

I Have Healed and Have New Energies Radiating From Me

Sara was glad to finally get some time for herself. It was a draining day at work, and she came home braced to get her kids to do their school assignments. But they had taken off to the neighbor's house for a birthday party. She was so glad to have got a couple of hours free. Having made herself an extra large latte, she settled on the couch, pretty pleased. Coming across a random Instagram post while scrolling snapped her into a somber mood. The post about the narcissistic behaviors of spouses sent her mind racing. Her mood flipped in an instant, and the coffee did not feel good all of a sudden. The next few hours went in a flash, wallowing in self-pity and a feeling of resentment. Sara's issue here is the emergence of automatic negative thoughts anytime, anywhere. Anything could trigger a rush of pain, self-pity, and helplessness. The solution is to figure out something simple and doable to handle this cascade.

Being in the Present Is the Secret to Harnessing My Positive Energies

Affirmations are a lot like getting into physical exercise. Regular, consistent efforts are the way to go if one wants to build muscles, increase flexibility, lose weight, or whatever your goal is. Just like nobody "feels" like working out regularly, affirmations also need conscious effort. The secret is to keep it small and doable but regular. Affirmations train our brains to build new neural pathways so that a certain attitude gets ingrained in us, which will slowly begin to reflect in our actions and decisions.

When I Walk Towards My Goal, the Forces of Life Rise to Meet Me Halfway

Life is unfair to the best of us; even the gods were not spared, and we know that. Without our fault, life will put us to the test, beat us, poke us, and rip us apart. Living in false bravado or living in denial is neither a solution nor a constructive countermeasure. When we accept the circumstance graciously, no matter how difficult it is, it becomes easier to look for solutions. Resistance causes us to feel resentful, angry, ashamed, and guilty. These limiting beliefs simply drag us further into suffering and gloom.

I Get That Every Challenge Is an Opportunity to Discover a Hidden Strength

This is where we need to initiate the next steps, which are fully in our control. We can not choose what happens to us, but we can choose our response. It is extremely challenging, the process is excruciatingly painful, and it will test our sanity, but it is possible. Sitting it out is worthwhile because the right knowledge is going to end the suffering. There will come the seemingly magical moment when the truth will free us. Empirical evidence in research suggests that our ability to reframe our problems builds our resilience and empowerment. That means we can mold our successes and challenges in ways that are advantageous to us.

I Realize That I Am Extraordinary

One is always welcome to walk down the beaten path. It is safe, and we need to spend less energy because we don't face resistance at every turn. Good affirmations in a weak mind are also an impotent formula. Affirmations to an immature person are like handing over the keys of a Ferrari to a teenager. But don't get me wrong here; it does not imply that every time something goes wrong, you are to blame, but it brings home the fact that responsibility is part of the package.

I Am Complete in Myself, and I Attract Strength From Around Me

Alia wished she had not been given the position. Every single moment since her appointment was spent with a strong sense of being an imposter. What she initially dismissed as the new job anxiety refused to disappear with time. *I am good at making a good impression, and it ends there. People will soon find out I am clumsy at the job.* She kept hearing these sentences over and over in her head, picking up instances of failures to reinforce the way she saw herself. Every time she was given an assignment, she would start to feel anxious. She would quickly run into dead ends in the process. She felt embarrassed to ask for assistance and ultimately quit after six months. She took up a job for which she was overqualified as her confidence hit an all-time low. This time, she kept the job because it was way less challenging. But it did nothing to improve her feeling of dissatisfaction because she knew she had way more potential than her work required.

I Function From a Place of Authenticity

At her new workplace, she met Greta, a charming lady in her fifties. She was the soul of the organization. She did not have fancy qualifications and rose through the ranks with sheer hard work. She was a natural leader and full of empathy. Her confidence in herself was unmistakable, and saw her through the most daunting of tasks. Greta was drawn to Alia's energy and took her under her wing. It did not take long for Greta to figure out Alia's self-defeating tendencies. She wished to help her out of her vicious cycle of self-sabotage. She encouraged Alia to initiate shifts in her mindset through positive affirmations that would act as an effective coping mechanism and reverse the downward spiral. This would alter Alia's perception of herself, which in turn would eventually influence her decision-making in all spheres of herself. Alia took the leap of faith because of her admiration for Greta. Seemingly simple affirmations, such as *I am capable*, played perpetually in her mind, and that was enough to reverse a lot of self-doubt. It was just the beginning of a new journey for Alia, and she knew there was no looking back.

I Love Spending Time With Myself

Goldie had emotional eating problems. Food was the straw in the ocean of life that she held onto for dear life. The stressor was mostly internal. On a perfectly good day, she would have struggled with self-doubts, and she would find reasons that justified her emotions. Therapy finally revealed that the unhealed child within her had spent too much time trying to read the energies of her mother to stay safe. All Goldie knows is that her mother was extremely unpredictable. Her smiling face would convert to boiling anger for reasons that were beyond Goldie's comprehension. Overthinking became a natural trait since she never learned to trust the natural process of life. She dreaded spending time with herself, and food appeared to be the only haven that kept her away from her inner demons.

Goldie was encouraged to spend time with herself to reconcile with the fact that she was complete in herself and needed no validation from anybody else in the world. Spending time alone is difficult for many of us until we find the root cause. It is easy to be busy, but being able to sit with ourselves without our thoughts going out of control is no ordinary feat, and Goldie was achieving it one moment at a time.

I Understand That Mistakes Are Part of an Important Process of Growth

Although her name was Queen, she had never felt like one. Her parents and the environment seemed to care little about her feelings as she recalled her early years of neglect and shame. She grew up with constant self-doubt and fog in her head, learning on the way, whatever it took to survive. She realized pleasing people was a strategy that worked to cover herself from her mother's harsh tongue. Her father did not bother to give her the emotional support she badly needed. She learned to feign that she was strong and capable of taking care of herself. Her dear grandma, who was around until she was 10 years old, was the only person who appeared happy that the Queen existed. Her granny's one statement, "Queen, you are a precious gift," stuck with her because that was the only nice thing she had ever heard about herself. That particular memory had not died despite being covered in an overwhelming quantity of negativity.

The Extraordinary Comes to Me When I Do Ordinary Things With Gratitude

When she was hired as a librarian after graduating, she felt liberated at last. Little did she realize her trauma would spill over into her new identity as well. One critical comment from her senior on the job was enough to derail her. She would go numb with resentment and not know how to take the feedback in good spirits. She was unable to look at mistakes as part of her growth. She would take it as a personal attack that questioned her worth. Her prior experiences would skew the comment and cause internal turmoil. It took her some time and the support of her bestie to help her stick to her positive affirmations of believing that she was good enough.

Nothing Is Stressful Unless I Believe It to Be

Although it seemed pointless, one evening, she decided to scan her memories for the good times of her life. She was surprised to see some lines on her notepad. Not bad! She persisted. At the end of the exercise, her grandma's statement seemed to surge and stand out. She intuitively felt that it was something that could withstand all the storms in her life. With time spent soaking in the positives, she began to get a certain strength and radiance back with that one statement. For starters, she began to recognize constructive criticism and separate it from offensive remarks. Next, she learned to stop reacting to negativity with her newfound assurance that she was perfectly okay. She looked forward to the time when she would be in a position to forgive everyone who hurt her. She owed it to herself to take the responsibility of cutting the vicious cycle and landing on fresh ground.

I Trust My Upbringing and the People Who Shaped Me Because It Is Not All About Me

Rehana was the first girl in her family to go to a University, an Ivy League one at that. All was good, but gradually the pressure of being a star performer began to take a toll on her ability to sustain her days. The overwhelming feeling of having to sail through her degree and land a good job led her into a complete meltdown in the final year of college. Nobody had a clue until the day she broke down in the lecture hall while waiting for her turn for the viva voce.

Rehana had to learn to let go. Sometimes, taking your hands off the steering wheel and not trying to control everything calms the nerves immediately. Great artists and creators believe that their masterpieces were not their making but made through them. Almost magically, this takes off the pressure of performance. It helps to have faith and show up, despite our skepticism. We need to focus on things under our control, such as integrity and hard work. The rest would fall in place when we are calm enough to allow things to happen right.

I'd Rather Be a Diamond With a Flaw Than Be a Pebble Without Any

Fayola clenched her fist every time she recollected her decision not to send the marketing proposal PowerPoint before the deadline. The design house she worked for would have got that massive opportunity to cut through the competition with that proposal. Fayola spent weeks with the research and got impressive insights. But at some point, she got obsessed with preparing the slides with statistical data. She unwittingly allowed perfection to come in the way of the good. Her bosses would have got the big picture anyways with the nitty-gritty of numbers. It was a gut-wrenching feeling for her when she later found out that the firm went ahead with a plan that was half as good as hers.

The temptation is too great to overcome. We discard the water for the elusive mirage only to end up with a busted fantasy. Much as we wish to come up with path-breaking ideas, it is the ability to make seemingly ordinary decisions in a sustained manner that keeps us going. We do not want to keep the diamond from sparkling just because there is a chip somewhere.

I See Abundance and Love Around Me

Much as we want to be in charge of our own lives, we cannot forget that life is full of pleasant surprises. Being in the driver's seat has its importance, but not at the cost of having the ability to chill out in the back seat when life demands so. If only we did not come in our way often.

Rini was in love with Tokyo. When her husband announced that they would need to move from Chicago a decade ago, she was completely unsettled. The idea of traveling with a newborn into a new country with an unfamiliar language and culture filled her with dread. But that was history, and the new land grew into her, and she came to love it like no other. Today, the thought of having to uproot herself from Tokyo was unthinkable. Her eyes welled up every time she thought of it. Her emotional outbursts and unpredictable moods were difficult for her and her family. That was when Rini realized that it was sometimes important to let go and let life take over. She was a more peaceful soul once the resistance stopped within.

I Am Thankful for the Criticisms That Have Helped Me Reset My Skills for the Better

Being tough and navigating people does not come easily and is a quality that cannot be taken for granted. It becomes a question of whipping up the right skills at the right time. When we are brought up in a trusting environment or where there is a lot of importance given to integrity, it does get traumatizing to thrive in a manipulating environment. But only initially. The new problem challenges us to figure out the right strategies and skill sets required to handle it and turn it in our favor. It is devastating when we are ignorant of the skill sets, but it is freeing and rewarding once we understand what is to be done. We reach the "aha" moment when we get spiritually, emotionally, and intellectually stronger. And there is no need to take revenge even though it gets tempting. Manipulators usually dig their graves. Looking back, we usually find that our tormentors have been our greatest teachers on the pathway to strength.

People Know Me as a Wise Person With a Sharp Wit

Not everyone liked Brenda. In case you thought she was worried about it, she was only happy about it. Slimy manipulators and gossipers found it frustrating to be around her. They would find that none of the politickings at the office affected her confidence. The harder they tried to put her down, the higher she seemed to be heading in dignity and demeanor. Her confidence only seemed to get stronger with each episode of rumor-mongering about her. The harshest thing for them to handle was that she would never confront them or get provoked at any point in time. It was almost as if they did not exist for her. This was only possible because Brenda was aware of her strengths. She spent her energy and time cultivating the right kind of friendships and developing worthwhile hobbies. She kept away from them in a strategic manner. She would elude them because she used her wit to keep her distance. They were not able to get information about her to use against her, and this got them frustrated.

I Dare to Let Go of My Unhelpful Patterns of Thinking... and Life Rewards Me With a New "Hello There!"

There are more times than we care to admit when our intelligence works against us. One would be pleasantly surprised to see life reward us with a fresh lease on life the moment we muster up the guts to discard our all-too-familiar thought processes.

Jane spent her childhood seeing her mother frustrated with a lot of things in life. Her mom was unhappy with her marriage, her failed career, her extended family, her neighbors, what not, and who not. Jane imbibed this attitude without being conscious of it. She found herself struggling in many areas of her life as she grew up. Much as she had her personality, the traits and attitudes she picked up due to her conditioning would manifest themselves at the most unexpected times. It took her a lot of time and experience to come to this realization. She began to watch her thoughts and keep things from getting complicated in her mind. Any difference of opinion with her husband would spin into a complicated plot, thanks to her childhood experience of trauma when her parents fought. She realized she was replaying the pattern in her head and taking for granted that her problems had to be long-drawn and mysteriously complicated. Once this realization set in, she was equipped to deal with issues in a smarter manner. She was able to now deploy her sense of humor, quick wit, and chutzpah in nipping problems in the bud. She was able to look at issues on merit and not box them in familiar patterns.

Life Moves in Synchronicity When Kept Fundamentally Simple

It struck Megan first when she was getting into her forties and generally getting a feeling that she was not able to keep up with her kids and many of her friends when it came to figuring out how gadgets worked. She would lose confidence every time someone showed impatience, be it while using the payment apps or getting the album of her choice on the music app. She had to keep herself from being redundant. Her epiphany came when she went to visit her grandma. The 95-year-old grand lady was on Facetime with her grandniece, who lived halfway around the world. Megan, taken aback, asked her how, and she waved her hand in the air and said, "Everything can be figured out. After all, it was invented to make life simple and not complicated. So, it's got to be simple. I remember how scared we were when we got the electric stove in the kitchen 80 years back. How silly it feels," she winked. Learn the simplest thing about something new and then go to the next simple thing. Eventually, you will realize you have that thing under your belt, no matter how complicated it looks. You will also realize that most people around you only have a superficial understanding of most things but speak like experts.

I Show That I Am Caring and Vulnerable

We construct walls at some point in life to keep ourselves safe, to appear tough, and to look unapproachable. The thing is that we forget to examine the relevance of those boundaries as life progresses and end up pushing the right people away from us in the process. Dimple's friends found her mom intimidating. Her stern look had them withdraw every time they bumped into her. Dimple's teenage years were filled with turmoil when she compared her mother's coldness with the friendly demeanor of her friends' mothers. Her assumptions of her mother's warmth affected their relationship for years to come. It did not change until decades later when Dimple understood the source of that cold demeanor, but then that wouldn't make up for the lost years. It does help to check our face now and then for those redundant walls, for showing our caring and vulnerable side is a sign of sure strength.

I Speak From a Place of Strength, Always

Sometimes the question is, "Whose truth?" The truth may not reveal itself at one's bidding but would ultimately find its way to unravel. I have begun many arguments, convinced I was right, to discover midway that it is not so simple. I hear either another point of view or the perspective of the person I am confronting, and there arises the opportunity to course correct. You will only earn the respect and gratitude of the person you are confronting when you play fair with your new position. You will find the adamant, unfair, immature, obnoxious other compelled to return the generosity.

When we question another person's actions or some unfavorable event in life, we are essentially putting up resistance and rejecting reality. Such resistance, in turn, causes the persistence of the situation. Try acceptance in its place, and you will find yourself catapulted to a position of strength.

I Like To Push My Boundaries of Possibilities Every Now and Then

Ruth seemed to have everything one would ask for. Every time she felt like opening her heart to someone, she got the feeling that they did not take her seriously. They would say, "How could you complain? You are so lucky, and you should be grateful." She was feeling choked in her entitlements that no longer made her feel worthy. She needed to do something else apart from managing her family business. She finally found the courage to set off to an obscure village to teach. Ruth permitted herself to upset her manicured life for a year. The time frame made the whole idea less overwhelming for her and those dependent on her. Experiencing contradictions in the form of poverty, lack of opportunities, the joy of simple living, and witnessing human resilience in the face of hardships all completely changed her perspective. No fancy degree had taught her the lessons life offered her. She felt herself grow and went back with a new will to use her resources and skills to change the lives of people around her. She finally had the conviction that she mattered and was capable of changing the world for the better. Her affirmations saw her through, helped her overcome her fears, and she got her purpose.

Affirmations like this help build a realistic world view. It makes making mistakes less traumatic and one feels safe experimenting with things. It helps one forgive oneself and the world to be able to start on a fresh note. It is the framework on which we navigate the known and the unknown to emerge safe and sound and learn meaningful lessons.

I trust and follow my spiritual path. ✽✽

I grow in body, mind, and soul. ✽✽

I welcome universal wisdom. ✽✽

I align with higher purpose. ✽

Chapter Seven:
SAMPLE ACTIVITIES AND BEST PRACTICES

eeßßßßee

"But affirmations don't seem to be working for me," we are likely to say in exasperation every once in a while.

Don't worry; it can be a thoroughly disappointing and strange experience when you are initiating the practice. It will make you feel all fake and foolish when uninitiated. Do you worry about sounding Pollyanna? The idea is not to walk around feeling excessively cheerful and optimistic all the time. That is equally toxic and unrealistic, and that is not the intent of affirmations. Misconceptions and a superficial understanding are factors that prevent us from getting to the essence.

Then one would think of emotional discipline. Are you up for it? Of course, you are! But the painful truth is that you are not going to change just because you read so many books or listen to brilliant podcasts. They help build perspective, but the action has to be yours to bring it alive. There is a world of difference between admiring a good dish and building the skills to make one. Consuming a fantastic show is not the same as creating a great one. We don't always realize that. Get up and write your script because the creator is within you. Do you want to wake up to this fact?

Rachel wished she could quit smoking. She had picked up the habit while at University, and she was in her 30s now. The fag was her one trusted anchor. It was with her through all her relationship affairs and breakups. It unconditionally helped her pull through research papers and high stake interviews and, without a doubt, got her to keep her sanity through the dog-eat-dog world of ambitions. Or so she believed. Her dependency on smoking had only increased every time she swore to quit. In her head, she knew this would land her in trouble someday. Her lungs were already showing signs of strain. She began to see a therapist to help her quit. She wanted to do her part to make the therapy work, and that's when she was advised to do self-talk. She started reciting her affirmations, telling herself she was healthy and that she was making modest changes every day. Slowly, she managed to give herself a four-hour non-smoking window. That made the task a lot less overwhelming. She managed to increase the space to a six-hour one in a few months. She was willing to consider a change, thanks to her daily affirmations. It helped her picture times when she could handle her business without using nicotine to calm her anxiety. She went from being a chain smoker to an evening smoker in just a year. She realized that there was a good chance of changing even that. Because her emotions and logic were in sync, she never missed a dose of medication or a session of behavioral therapy. Daily affirmations served as the fuel that enabled things to occur.

Why Do Our Emotions Get the Better of Us?

As you read this page, someone somewhere is hurting in the mind; millions of minds are hurting. Nothing else could be more certain in society. We feel challenged, and our peace is threatened at every corner. It could be a mean remark by a boss, a careless statement by a good friend, a racist slur, a prejudiced government policy, the expectations of society that you are resisting, your partner letting you down when you ask for support, children who don't seem to like you, or an anxious friend you cannot seem to be of help. It could be one problem at a time or a cascade of multiple problems that threaten to break your spirit forever. Sometimes it is tempting to just give up. The excruciating pain of being alive becomes impossible to bear, and you don't see hope anywhere.

That's exactly at that point, my friend, when something sparks from deep within the spirit. There is a voice that assures you that you are fine, even though everyone else is blaming, shaming, or bemoaning your situation. You will see no reason to believe that tiny voice. The brain will give you enough reasons and logic to push it away. The soft, timid voice will appear to stand no chance to the powerful negativity. You will seek comfort in self-pity and in harboring the victim mentality. People take to alcohol and resort to substance use to numb the pain that is tearing them apart.

We need to know that we have our thought patterns. The trouble is that we don't realize that we have them. We appear to be reacting and responding to people in particular and life in general, but we need to know that we do so in a pattern. This pattern is in itself a complex maze nurtured by upbringing and culture and resides in the subconscious realm. So when someone says something, our interpretation depends on the filter through which it passes. This explains why many times, a seemingly harmless statement by the speaker can wreak havoc in the mind of the receiver. It is better to reconcile to the fact that you have an elephant as your pet now. It has its own will, is stronger than you, and does not like to listen. Your task as the owner is to tame it, so all the rules of taming a wild elephant will therefore apply. How about getting some training advice from the pet store, yeah? It's a lousy one, but nonetheless!

Journal Prompts

It would not appeal to your intellect, but your mind needs it. Compare it to building muscles. It happens only when you work out. Having a doctorate in physical education will not help convert fat to muscle. Orienting your energy to achieve specific outcomes is like training your guns at a target. You benefit, period. Interestingly, it is easy to put habits in place when it comes to affirmations. Only for individuals who practiced good affirmation hygiene have they been effective. That is the simple truth. Reading material about how they work will encourage you but will not do the task for you. After carefully examining a large number of practitioner-reported anecdotes, we can safely say that daily repeats over several months are a crucial component of success.

Journaling has been used for centuries by us to achieve peace of mind. There have been many studies to show how journaling increased optimism and gratitude, helped ease anxiety, boosted resilience, and overcame intense emotions, resulting in fewer negative emotions to stressors (Baikie et al., 2012). Always remember that there is no right or wrong way of writing. Let it flow and unravel the magic. Julia Cameron talks about how the morning pages are meant to provoke, clarify, comfort, cajole, prioritize, and synchronize the day at hand (Cameron, n.d.). She talks of it as a clearing exercise where you face your devils and do not spend the rest of the day running away from them.

An Exquisite-Looking Journal — Because, in time, it will begin speaking to you. When you are doing something of weight and worth, the place you record it should reflect its relevance. Engaging your sense of touch and sight will surely hold the wandering mind in place. Leave no stone unturned—you are playing to win. It is also established that writing by hand engages the brain conceptually as compared to typing.

Have a Time and Place for the Deliberations—That is sacred, and no one, not even you, should be allowed to take it away. Choose a time that suits you and a place that resonates, and stick to the ritual with a vengeance. That is your bedrock on which you can let the affirmations flow in peace.

Repetition Serves to Strengthen—Writing one affirmation multiple times forces you to relive it again and again. It gets etched in all corners of your consciousness and beyond. Hearing it as you say them aloud further cements the intention, leaving no room for escape. But do not expect instant results. Stick it out to see the profound turn of events for yourself. Missing the climax after all the hard work will be a pity, and you will only be standing in your way.

The Language—If the goal is time-bound and specific, then the affirmation ought to reflect this. Saying "I am good at learning languages" will not help as much as "I am capable of doing the language test by December." Avoidant terms do not sit well. Replacing *I will not neglect my needs with I will take care of my needs* makes it straightforward because of the presence of the word care in place of neglect. There are rigid rules, though. As long as something feels authentic to you, go ahead with confidence. Try it out and decipher the best way to make it work.

PROMPTS THAT WILL HELP YOU
GET STARTED

Relationships

What are the strengths of this relationship
in your view?

Can the cultural meaning attributed to this
relationship be reframed?

Identify the troubling areas and define the
parts that no longer serve you.

Are your responses helping you in
achieving a win-win?

What are the boundaries I need to establish
to keep it healthy?

How do you want to inspire others around
you?

How can I demonstrate compassion?

What are the non-negotiable values in this
relationship?

How do I demonstrate my likes and
dislikes?

Career

What do I aspire to demonstrate at work?

Does my communication style inspire trust?

Do I project the right combination of
warmth and strength?

Where do you find fulfillment?

Is the financial incentive coming at the cost
of finding purpose in the role?

What do I need to unlearn?

What are the skills I need to imbibe?

What are the aspects of work that
overwhelm me?

Can I reframe my issues to find a better
solution?

What is coming in the way of making me
feel empowered?

Spiritual Growth

What is preventing me from seeking fulfillment in the present environment?

How do I know myself better?

How do I figure out my strengths and purpose?

Is my conditioning dwarfing my potential?

Do others find inspiration in me?

Ambitions and Desires

How can I do this differently?

What can I learn from others?

What should I unlearn?

Managing Conflicts

What are the things that cause intense
anger or resentment?

What can I do when life gets unfair?
What are my strategic options?

Am I suppressing my sadness?

What are my choices in venting out my
emotions bottled up inside me?

What are things that provoke me? How
can I respond and not react?

What are the automatic negative
thoughts that spring out of my thoughts
regularly?

What am I afraid of?

What are the negative self-stories I have
created in my mind?

What can I do to overcome the self-
defeating patterns in me?

Visualization

Bethy would often see herself on the ramp. She was pursuing a master's in business administration but could not shake off the desire to be a model on the catwalk. She would bring the work of designers to life, and she would feel on top of the world. But there was no way she could figure out the means to achieve her goal. Her parents actively discouraged her from going into the fashion industry, she did not have the money to build a portfolio, and she did not have the network that could somehow lead her to an assignment. But every morning, she saw herself walking gracefully on the ramp. Four years later, we know Bethy to be a successful model with an envious portfolio. The means, the networking, the opportunities, and her choices had all rearranged themselves to align with what she saw. It was hard work, no doubt, but she had the contentment of having earned all of it well, and that is all that mattered.

We need to dissect the progress to understand what went on in Bethy's life. The desire within her had to be channeled for it to see the light of day. Otherwise, it was very easy for the dream to get overpowered by other options. Bethy's journey of reining in her energy and getting it to achieve a certain outcome is something a lot of us tend to overlook. The reason can be attributed to the fact that we have never been taught to harvest that power within us. The power of visualization is used by elite achievers, and we tend to miss it because of a lack of orientation. Visualization puts your goals on track and accelerates them by activating your creativity and programming the mind to attract what you desire.

The Technique for Practice

Close your eyes to imagine yourself in the time and place of having achieved what you want. All your senses have lived that moment where you hear, see, smell, taste, and feel the result. Go on, daydream. Start by seeing the moment like an audience member and proceed to then embody the person you can see in your mind.

Open your eyes to the new reality of being that person from that moment onwards because your mind has already seen it happen. If you visualize being a successful entrepreneur, you will start organizing your workspace, picking up the right skills, networking with the right people, dressing up like one, and being responsible like one. Your familiar old habits may tempt you to go back to them, but now you know why you need to change. You would need to repeat it every day because, remember, you are training an elephant.

If you serve an elephant the same fruits every day, it will get bored quickly. Add variety to keep the enthusiasm. Create goal cards with quotations, make cards with original artwork, have handy cutouts of your role models, make lists, photo files, or anything else you can think of to track your progress toward a new professional path, fitness objective, or lifestyle change.

By visualizing your goal every single day, you will be serving your mind with a purpose supported by rehearsals that keep it off distractions. Our willpower, energy, and time are finite resources. We need to deploy them with care. Betty used Photoshop to make images of herself on the catwalk with the hottest designers. She had these images all over the place: in her room, pocketbook, laptop screen saver, journal, you name it. She saw herself approaching agents for work, she saw herself getting rejected, and she saw herself getting up every time she fell. She had done it so much in her mind that real experiences no longer intimidated her.

Elephants need discipline, though. It needs to look at those cards and admire those photoshopped pictures, even on the days it feels lousy or demotivated. The rider needs to remind it that she is in charge.

Your visualization ought to carry along your values too. Achieving something at any cost will leave you feeling miserable deep within, and it will not be an easy journey from thereon.

One would gradually begin to get conscious of the impact of their everyday choices and subconsciously align it to their goals. From shoes to attitude, your choices will begin to speak a new language. You find yourself rejecting things that don't align with your goals and putting yourself out there where you want to be.

One important caveat, though: Visualization serves its purpose only when done in deliberation for the specific time frame you have devoted to it every day. You would need to let go of it and then live in the moment the rest of the time. Letting it overtake your real moments will lead to you living in denial and make you a slave of your mind.

Mindfulness

At the end of the day, life is a lot more than our dreams and precision constructs. When we get too consumed by our ideas of what we want to be, we end up not being open to surprises. Sometimes, failing to achieve our dreams also is the best thing that happens to us. Ambition and letting go both have their places. Learning to savor life for whatever it offers, sweet or bitter, teaches us humility and acceptance. The route to peace is surrender too, and discretion always is the better part of valor.

While wisdom tells us that we are in our best state of mind when we can live in the present and savor the moment, our minds are either ruminating in the past or the imagined future. We lock ourselves up and wonder why we suffer.

Mindfulness is the state where we are aware and nonjudgmental of things as they are. This awareness is not automatic and has to be brought in with purpose. With mindfulness, we gain the ability to approach a situation with openness by switching off the autopilot mode of thinking. While meditation requires you to sit down in a place, mindfulness is practiced in every moment as you go about your day.

Techniques of Mindfulness

Make it a habit of snapping back as you go about your day. Of course, your mind will resist. It loves to brood about the past and the future. It is not your fault because, remember, it is your pet elephant that follows you everywhere. Take a second off to be aware of your body touching the chair that is supporting you.

Take another moment to listen to that bird chirping on the tree near your window. Yes, there is no apparent "purpose" to it; it only helps us become unstuck from the incessant train of thought.

It is not about forcibly controlling your mind, but the opposite. It is about allowing thoughts to come in but then letting them go without holding on or identifying with them. You will learn to look at your thoughts like an unaffected outsider and begin to see your patterns. Getting untangled is precisely the purpose.

Accept every emotion that is bothering you because that is the first step to loosening its hold on you. It can disturb you to accept situations as they are. Go on and define them in words: "I am angry" or "I am feeling defeated." Acknowledge the feelings and the sensations it triggers in your body. Be aware of them without getting sucked into them. Just notice. No action, no judgment. Muster the courage because the journey of transition will kick start from here.

We use the breath as the symbol of the present. Getting your attention to your breath, again and again, is your sure-shot way to get back to the present. We will use this method of bringing attention to the breath as the formula to focus attention on everything else that deserves your attention. Of course, the mind will resist and wander because that's its job; you cannot blame yourself for it or get frustrated. You need to keep calmly reminding it that you are in charge by bringing attention back to the breath.

By bringing in awareness, we slowly realize that our thoughts are not facts and are influenced by our emotions, conditioning, and our tendencies. We step outside of them, and they no longer have their grip on us. You are now in a position to control them and replace them with your desired affirmations.

Meditation

Dr. Joe Dispenza (Vibrant Life, 2021) talks of how meditating on the kind of personality you want to become wires and fires the connections in the brain to make one conscious of their unconscious thoughts. This further gives you the scope to discard unhelpful thoughts and replace them with new thoughts. Repeating the exercise of meditating on your aspired personality then becomes the subconscious program that will set in a cascading effect on the choices, feelings, and experiences we have daily. Meditation, most importantly, allows us to let go. The wisdom of letting go and letting things be will reveal unimaginable peace, something we have no idea could even exist.

Perspective-building is aided by meditation. Because we are so preoccupied with our issues, the world itself seems small in comparison. We seem to live in our heads all the time, and to us, we appear to be the most significant thing, and our thoughts seem to be more important than everything else. Fundamentally, the practice of meditation helps us recognize how small we and our issues are—all but an eensy speck of life floating on a tiny mass of land and water floating in endless space—and liberates us from our own trap. Meditation empowers one by acknowledging that solutions to our problems lie within us and that our autonomy need not be entrusted to an outside source.

Techniques of Meditation

It begins with the idea of being with yourself. Find a peaceful place without distractions. Close your eyes and do nothing. If you are feeling overwhelmed, slightly open your eyes and look at the ground in front of you. Thoughts will flood in; do not resist. We need to accept that wandering is the nature of the mind. But do not get sucked into any particular thought. Watch them as an observer would do.

Being able to sit quietly does not come easily to many people. If you are uncomfortable, replace the act of sitting by going alone for a stroll, stretching, or a solitary activity like painting. You will gradually be able to spend time with yourself.

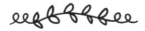

Keep bringing your attention to your breath and observe the inhaling and exhaling actions as they happen involuntarily. The thoughts will not stop, but slowly your attachment to them will get lesser and lesser. That's when your win begins.

Repetition is key in meditation. Meditating for 15 minutes each in the mornings and evenings will help in centering you to a peaceful state of being.

Mediation, as easy as the instructions sound, just does not come easily for the uninitiated. So please do not get disheartened by failures. Trying too hard, setting deadlines, looking for signs of progress, and seeking extrinsic motivation will not take us anywhere. Self-awareness sometimes takes time to surface, so patience is a prerequisite. Taking one-on-one guidance from experts and practicing in the presence of a teacher are great ideas to get initiated and get one to stick to the practice.

Nothing can dim the light that shines from within.

MAYA ANGELOU

CONCLUSION

With the rider of our mind convinced of the ways of tough nut affirmations, it is now up to us to train the elephant. With gentle yet firm hands, we will cajole and convince, show tough love one step at a time, every single day, so that we have a giant yielding to us with the smoothness of silk. The journey of affirmations is that of being part of the solution and not lending ourselves to be paralyzed by problems within and beyond our control. I remember vividly the phases of my life, walking through with a cloud lodged in my mind. Days would come and go with me latching on without any sense of purpose. The phenomenon could repeat in the future too. But the difference would be that I would have tools to deploy to tide through the uncertainties.

If the unfair treatment comes from our intimate relationships, the suffering gets insidious, and when it comes from society, it appears unsurmountable. The first step to addressing this is understanding that the other is far from perfect. Individuals and societies are carrying their baggage of past trauma with them. It is not your fault that they know no better than to treat you so. Once you realize that the action is coming from a place of fear, insecurity, guilt, shame, and ignorance, you are in a position to choose the response. Instincts will direct us to respond from the same level of negativity. The outcome will be a sure-shot conflict of interest, similar to when two cars collide. However, visualize your vehicle moving on a higher lane starting from a position of strength, positivity, and compassion. Because you are not even in the same lane, there won't be a collision. Not only that but every time you go to a higher lane, the vehicle in the lower lane slows down because it has no incentive for collision. Affirmations are your fuel for the higher lane.

The Region-Beta Paradox explains the human response to misery. The theory explains the reason we all choose to stay in a state of acceptable levels of discomfort rather than take the initiative to come out of it unless it changes to a state of intense discomfort. The funny result of this phenomenon is that we have a better chance of getting out of a problem when it is intense than when it is mild. In other words, a frog put in hot water will have a better chance of surviving than a frog swimming in water that is gradually heating up. The first case forces the frog to take action, while in the second case, the need to jump out is just not felt.

We lead our lives much like the second frog. We know what is to be done but cannot bring ourselves to do it. We will remain with that dissatisfied partner, entrepreneur, or employee and continue to suffer, and take action to change the status only when there is a compelling need to do so, and that emergency never occurs. Deploying willpower alone to change is not enough and will only exhaust us. We need some other trick up our sleeves. How does one stay out of Region-Beta so that we don't live with regrets? The immediate step is to recognize that we are in the middle of one. Then we address the mild problem with mild consistency to beat it at its own game. It could even involve taking unsure but tiny steps on a new path with your affirmations to protect you.

We have been talking about the self through and through. It's been about self-affirmations, self-esteem, and self-confidence. Let's zoom out a bit to put the "self" in context so that we see clearly where the self fits. Each one of us is part of a larger whole. We thrive when we bond, when our families and tribe feel protected and there for each other. We need to be centered, but not at the cost of losing the big picture of integration. We also need to constantly remind ourselves that it is okay to share our pains and happiness and seek support from fellow human beings.

"Ted Williams, Michael Jordan, Yo-Yo Ma, Mozart... And they had some other traits in common. They had this drive to fail. They had this notion that every day they were going to go out on the baseball field or into the practice room or the gym, and they were going to push themselves beyond their limits, and then they were going to study that part that wasn't quite working and trying to figure out how they could improve it, kind of welcoming failure into their lives instead of running away and shrinking from that failure," said author David Shenk (2011), explaining how geniuses are made and not born. Imagine following this rule in everything we set out to do.

Looking closely into every culture brings to the surface its esoteric principles of harnessing the power of the mind. Some make it to the headlines, while many are shrouded in mystery, waiting to catapult onto the world stage. Jose Silvadoros, a Mexican-American of humble origins, is a cult figure of sorts in the modern world. He stumbled upon techniques that could hyperpower the mind, all this when trying to get his children to perform better at their studies. The Silva technique is a beacon for hundreds of thousands of its followers to enhance their creative and intuitive powers. People have used his techniques to manifest their affirmations. The brain apparently enters into a particular state of functioning called the alpha state of awareness. Such possibilities, though met with both skepticism and intense faith, only showcase that the human mind is still a deep mystery waiting to be solved. An open mind, a questioning mind, and faith are all but different lenses for approaching its vastness. The point is to keep seeking and refusing to settle for any particular viewpoint.

Interestingly, affirmations don't just do the work of adding aspects to our life to make it better. It is as much about eliminating aspects that don't resonate with us anymore. It is all about choosing to keep only things that matter and deliberately rejecting the trivials that eat into our energy. We end up becoming better versions when clutter is removed regularly. I wish that you continue to dialogue with the book and take it to heart. Tell the book every day about the steps you took to make your life a wee bit different, and every day it will give you more. Like Jonathan Haidt (2006) said, "We might have already encountered the Greatest Idea, the insight that would have transformed us had we savored it, taken it to heart, and worked it into our lives."

SHARE YOUR INSIGHTS

I hope you've enjoyed your journey through *Badass Affirmations for Women*. Your perspective is invaluable.

If you could take a moment to leave an honest review, I would greatly appreciate it. Your thoughts will not only guide others in deciding if this is the right choice for them but will also help me to continue creating content that you find valuable.

Your opinion matters, and I'm eager to hear about your experience. Thank you for being a part of this journey and for sharing your insights.

I am deliberate and
afraid of nothing.

AUDRE LORD

REFERENCES

A *quote by Rumi*. (n.d.). Goodreads. www.goodreads.com/quotes/551027-yesterday-i-was-clever-so-i-wanted-to-change-the

Ahern, H. M. (n.d.). *Mindfulness based stress reduction handbook*. U&Counselling. https://www.dcu.ie/sites/default/files/students/mindfulness_based_stress_reduction_handbook.pdf

Akbari, K. (2023, April, 2). *31 positive affirmations for imposter syndrome*. Eye Mind Spirit. https://www.eyemindspirit.com/post/31-healing-affirmations-for-imposter-syndrome

Baikie, K. A., Geerligs, L., & Wilhelm, K. (2012). Expressive writing and positive writing for participants with mood disorders: An online randomized controlled trial. *Journal of Affective Disorders, 136*(3), 310–319, https://doi.org/10.1016/j.jad.2011.11.032

Botton, S. (2023, July 5). *This is 55: María Luisa Arroyo Cruzado responds to the Oldster Magazine Questionnaire*. Oldster Magazine. https://oldster.substack.com/p/this-is-55-maria-luisa-arroyo-cruzado

Cameron, J. (n.d.). *Morning Pages*. Julia Cameron Live. https://juliacameronlive.com/basic-tools/morning-pages/

Canfield, J. (2018,November 13.) *Visualization techniques to affirm your desired outcomes: A step-by-step guide*. LinkedIn. https://www.linkedin.com/pulse/visualization-techniques-affirm-your-desired-outcomes-jack-canfield/

Cascio, C. N., O'Donnell, M. B., Tinney, F. J., Lieberman, M. D., Taylor, S. E., Strecher, V. J., & Falk, E. B. (2016). Self-affirmation activates brain systems associated with self-related processing and reward and is reinforced by future orientation. *Social Cognitive and Affective Neuroscience, 11*(4), 621–629. https://doi.org/10.1093/scan/nsv136

Cohen, G. L., & Sherman, D. K. (2014). The psychology of change: Self-affirmation and social psychological intervention. *Annual Review of Psychology, 65*(1), 333–371. https://doi.org/10.1146/annurev-psych-010213-115137

Contrarian Thinking. (n.d.). *Welcome, Contrarian.* Retrieved July 6, 2023, from https://contrarianthinking.co/thankyou-new/

Easton, D. (2016, December 9). *5 guidelines for dealing with difficult behaviors.* Kent State University. https://www.kent.edu/yourtrainingpartner/5-guidelines-dealing-difficult-behaviors

Easton, D. (2016, October 5). *The #1 way to control emotions during conflict: Focus on the issue.* Kent State University. https://www.kent.edu/yourtrainingpartner/1-way-control-emotions-during-conflict-focus-issue

Evans, H. (2019, October 23). *Why I write affirmations daily and why you should too.* Medium. https://medium.com/swlh/why-i-write-affirmations-daily-and-why-you-should-too-4ff8ae69d82

Haidt, J. (2006). *The happiness hypothesis: Putting ancient wisdom and philosophy to the test of modern science.* Arrow.

Heath, C., & Heath, D. (2010). *Switch: How to change things when change is hard.* Crown Business.

Housel, M. (2020). *The psychology of money: Timeless lessons on wealth, greed, and happiness.* Harriman House.

Invitational theory and practice: A framework for positive school. (n.d.). StudyLib. Retrieved July 6, 2023, from https://studylib.net/doc/9841255/invitational-theory-and-practice-a-framework-for-positive

Kahneman, D. (2011). *Thinking, fast and slow.* Farrar, Straus and Giroux.

Lieberman, D. E. (2020). *Exercised: The science of physical activity, rest and health.* Allen Lane.

Neffinger, J., & Kohut, M. (2014). *Compelling people: The hidden qualities that make us influential.* Plume.

Official Proverbs 31 Ministries. (2022, October 27). *Therapy & theology: The part emotional abuse plays in silencing women* [Video]. YouTube. https://youtu.be/uKwPh3ccwfE

Patel, B. (2023, April 12). *The Region-Beta Paradox and its impact on product and experimentation thinking.* Medium. https://productcoalition.com/the-region-beta-paradox-and-its-impact-on-product-and-experimentation-thinking-a97488dadb73

Purkey, W. W., & Stanley, P. H. (2002). The self in psychotherapy. *Humanistic Psychotherapies: Handbook of Research and Practice.*, 473–498. https://doi.org/10.1037/10439-015

Raypole, C. (2021, May 17). *Ready, set, journal! 64 journaling prompts for self-discovery.* Psych Central. https://psychcentral.com/blog/ready-set-journal-64-journaling-prompts-for-self-discovery#the-journal-prompts

Robinson, S. (2022). A case study of self-affirmations in teacher education. *Journal of Invitational Theory and Practice, 20,* 27–36. https://doi.org/10.26522/jitp.v20i.3734

Sanchez, C. (n.d.). *Contrarian Thinking.* Retrieved from https://www.codiesanchez.com/

Shenk, D. (2011). *The genius in all of us: New insights into genetics, talent, and IQ.* Knopf Doubleday Publishing GroupAnchor Books.

Sites, B & Davis, T. (n.d.). *Positive affirmations: Definition, examples, and exercises.* The Berkeley Well-Being Institute. https://www.berkeleywellbeing.com/positive-affirmations.html

Soo, S. (2023, March 22). *This 40-year-old introvert makes $2 million a year — 3 things she always does to "look and feel more confident."* CNBC Make It. https://www.cnbc.com/2023/03/22/i-run-a-2-million-business-and-i-am-an-introvert-here-are-my-tips-to-looking-and-feeling-confident.html

Steele, C. M. (1988). The psychology of self-affirmation: Sustaining the integrity of the self. *Advances in Experimental Social Psychology, 21*, 261–302. https://doi.org/10.1016/S0065-2601(08)60229-4

Taleb, N. N. (2012). *Antifragile: How to live in a world we don't understand.* Random House.

Taleb, N. (n.d.). *10 principles to live an antifragile life.* Farnam Street. https://fs.blog/an-antifragile-way-of-life/#:~:text=What%20is%20Antifragility

The Science of Affirmations. (2020, October 20). Monroe Wellness. https://www.monroewellness.com/post/the-science-of-affirmations#:~:text=Affirmations%20work%20by%20changing%20your

Valuetainment. (2019, September 3). *Do daily affirmations work?* [Video]. YouTube. https://www.youtube.com/watch?v=4gx9QrdqBBs

Vibrant Life. (2021, April 11). *Create new personality | Dr. Joe Dispenza | Personality improvement* [Video]. YouTube. https://www.youtube.com/watch?v=5JYPFqZVwQw&t=1s

What is the Silva Method? (n.d.). The Silva Method. https://www.silvamethod.com/

YouAreCreaters. (2017, January 11). *Change your life with these 10 affirmations! (Learn this)* [Video]. YouTube. https://www.youtube.com/watch?v=OOKTOrx1bDs

Made in the USA
Middletown, DE
25 November 2023

43532121R00073